Simple Ayurvedic

recipes

A COMPANION COOKBOOK TO FREEDOM IN YOUR RELATIONSHIP WITH FOOD

Myra Lewin

TABLE OF CONTENTS

ACKNOWLEDGEMENTS

I invite students to live in my home and experience Ayurveda firsthand during retreats and trainings. This book emerged out of my students' encouragement—from watching them write down the recipes as we ate.

My deepest appreciation goes to Patsy Mennuti, Kelsey Brusnyk, and Shannon Wianecki for their dedication to learning new ways and supporting me with this book.

I offer my respect and reverence to the many brilliant beings that brought forth the teachings of Ayurveda so that we may find a better way in this world.

INTRODUCTION

Cooking and eating are sacred acts, reminders that humanity, nature, and food are all one. They are powerful forms of nurturing and nourishment. Ayurveda, a five-thousand-year-old science of living, suggests preparing and eating food as an offering to the Divine. Ayurvedic practitioners have long recognized that food is a gift for longevity and healthy living. Reviving a respectful relationship to food brings richness and depth into day-to-day living, something that seems to be shortchanged these days.

My first book, *Freedom in Your Relationship with Food*, introduces the basic principles of Ayurveda and discusses the emotional components of eating. It explains individual constitution including the five elements, the doshas (vata, pitta, kapha), agni (digestive fire), and the gunas (sattva, rajas, tamas). These are all aspects of nature contained both within food and us. They directly affect the mind, body, and spirit of the consumer.

Ayurveda is both a nature-based science and an art of living. My experience with it has been extraordinary. It has empowered me to live a full life. This book arises from my own practice and information gleaned from many learned people in Ayurveda, including Dr. Sunil Joshi, Dr. David Frawley, Saraswati Burhman, Dr. Robert Svoboda, and many others. Use these pages to assist you in your own journey.

Simple Ayurvedic Recipes is filled with recipes focusing on balanced eating and easy approaches to food preparation. I made the decision not to put pictures of food in this book in hopes that it will awaken your creativity. Preparing food for yourself and others is meant to be an expression of your love and an exercise in learning to trust your internal guidance. It is not something to be measured against an ideal. Most importantly, I hope this book inspires you to bring the sacred into your meals and into your life.

∽

DEFINING GOOD HEALTH

Ayurveda refers to good health as balance, "knowingness" that all is well. Good health is reflected by:

- ⑥ A balanced appetite without cravings

- ⑥ Easy digestion without belching, bloating, or discomfort of any sort

- ⑥ Easy and regular elimination of urine, feces, sweat, and tears

- ⑥ A clear voice, bright eyes, and clear skin

- ⑥ Steady energy, emotions, and enthusiasm for life

- ⑥ A calm, pain-free body and mind

How does one cultivate and maintain such balance? Become familiar with your primary dosha(s) and the foods and lifestyle that are best for you. Learn how to keep your digestive fire strong. Work to eliminate even the smaller aggravation, or imbalance. Along with my previous book, Freedom in Your Relationship with Food, many resources exist. Consulting with a qualified practitioner or Ayurvedic doctor is an excellent way to continue on your path.

Whether this approach is a big change or a small change, let yourself enjoy the process. Release fears and have fun with it!

If you would like to share your experiences and experiments, contact us at halepule.com. See the Library of Self Healing in the Resource tab for links to sources for great tools.

∽

AUGMENTING AND EXTRACTIVE: KEYS TO BALANCE

You can enhance your well-being dramatically with proper proportions of the augmenting and extractive qualities of your meals.

Augmenting foods are nourishing, nurturing, and grounding. They add to the body, enhancing vitality. For example, cooked rice or sweet potatoes are augmenting. Extractive foods are cleansing in nature, drawing things out. This means they ask the body to give up something to digest food. Digesting extractive foods breaks down the essential fats needed for healthy function. They result in a lighter feeling in the body. They are appropriate in proper proportion with augmenting foods. Kale and beans are examples of extractive foods.

Very simply, balanced meals include slightly more augmenting (60%) than extractive (40%) foods.

Ayurveda suggests incorporating all six tastes: sweet, salty, sour, bitter, pungent, and astringent in each meal. (See *Freedom in Your Relationship with Food* for more information on the six tastes.) Augmenting foods contain more of the sweet, salty, and sour tastes. Extractive foods are predominantly bitter, pungent, and astringent. The recipes in this book are labeled according to this definition. Some are

labeled with both characteristics; one may be more promi-
nent than the other.

Consuming meals that are slightly more augmenting
than extractive will help you maintain a calm, balanced
state of body and mind. Even for cleansing protocols, a
certain amount of augmenting food is necessary to maintain stability while purification takes place. In your daily life,
work with a ratio of 60 to 40 percent, or 55 to 45 percent,
augmenting to extractive, and see how you feel. Extremes
in either direction over time will cause imbalance, leading
to disease.

A diet of primarily extractive foods will aggravate *vata
dosha*, resulting in symptoms such as:

- fear
- anxiety
- dry skin and or hair
- stiffness in the body including the joints and muscles
- disturbed sleep
- cold hands, cold feet
- feeling overwhelmed
- difficulty finishing things
- dehydration
- snap, crackle, pop in the joints
- difficulty focusing
- constipation
- overly talkative
- being secretive and self destructive
- tendency toward addictions

These complaints, among others, are common these days. One of the main causes is too much dry, light, airy, and refined food, and not enough high quality, juicy, unctuous, and augmenting food.

When you understand the augmenting or extractive qualities of foods, you can easily substitute one item for another while maintaining balance in a meal. Balanced meals are truly satisfying, and eliminate the need for snacking.

~

PRANA

Prana is life force. It is present in all living things and available to us as energy in the food we consume. Ideally we would eat food with the highest level of *prana*. A plant's *prana* begins deteriorating after it is picked. Freshly harvested and prepared foods offer the greatest life force. Food is best for you when its sattvic nature, or natural balance, is retained as long as possible. Cooking food wakes up its inherent *prana* and renders it digestible for humans.

~

SATTVA, RAJAS, AND TAMAS

Ayurveda regards the *gunas*: *sattva, rajas,* and *tamas* as tools to restore and maintain balance. *Sattva* represents equilibrium or balance, *rajas* is activity and agitation, and *tamas* is inertia. Each of the *gunas* is present in the mind and in everything you consume. The relative amount of each of these energies is continually shifting in the body and mind depending on what you consume through all of your senses. For example, very loud music is *rajas* and listening to it will create that state in your mind. Food that is cooked and left for days is *tamas*; the life force is depleted. Consuming primarily *sattvic* food influences your state of mind toward harmony and balance.

෮

DIGESTIVE FIRE (AGNI)

The digestive fire, or *agni*, is the energy within you that transforms what you consume into consciousness. How and what you eat, as well as your attitude and acceptance in life, affects your *agni*. *Agni* is responsible for the digestion, absorption, distribution, and elimination of what you eat and drink. It includes the enzymes and metabolic processes of digestion. The state of your metabolism is a result of the strength of your *agni*. Slightly stronger or weaker *agni* is associated with each person's unique constitution. However, everyone can have adequate *agni* with proper diet and lifestyle. Beyond your emotions, what and how you eat has the largest affect on the strength of your *agni*. Taking care of your *agni* will strengthen your immunity and mental stability.

෮

THE PERFECT PORTION

Knowing how much to eat is important. Overeating in any one sitting weakens your digestive fire, dulls your mind, and creates an accumulation of metabolic toxins, or *ama*, in your body.

Ayurvedic texts suggest how to determine your own perfect portion: at any meal, eat only what can be held in both hands cupped together. This can be difficult to judge depending on the type of food. For example, the difference between a handful of uncooked greens and a handful of cooked beans is significant. Another approach suggested in the texts is to consume 1/3 liquid, 1/3 food, and leave 1/3 for the gases to move things through. The condition of the digestive tract and the mind on any given day factors significantly in how effective these tools can be.

Nature also equipped humans with a built-in signal from the body to know when to stop eating: a subtle belch. If you eat slowly and chew each bite thoroughly, you will notice a small burp or release of air. Your body is giving you a message that it is full. The belch says: "stop eating now, I can't handle anymore."

Each time you ignore this natural indicator and continue eating, you are overeating. Overeating weakens *agni*. At the following meal, the weakness will be reflected in an earlier belch. When you eat beyond the belch, undigested food collects in your digestive tract where it ferments and becomes metabolic toxins. Eventually these toxins migrate into deeper tissues of the body and cause disease. Stop eating at the first belch and prevent future illness.

Many people say they don't belch. Usually this is because they eat too fast or unconsciously. Engaging in excess conversation while eating or feeling anxious and nervous around meal times causes tension in the diaphragm and belly. This will either impede or precipitate the belch and disturb your digestion. Relax yourself with some calm breathing before and during meals; the belch will come naturally. Eating in silence is quite beneficial.

With a little investigation everyone who claims they don't belch, has found that they do!

HELPFUL TIPS

These tips will help make Ayurvedic food preparation and eating an enjoyable and balanced experience.

⚬ Only cook with ingredients grown and processed without the use of chemicals.

⚬ If you cannot find the ingredients you want, ask your local grocery or farmer to consider carrying them. Customer requests help store buyers and farmers know what their customers want.

⚬ Run creative energy and love during food preparation and eating! Learn to do this with the guided Subtle Energy Meditations in *Freedom in Your Relationship with Food* or *halepule.com*.

APPLIANCES & COOKWARE

Explore different materials for plates and utensils, such as wood and porcelain rather than stainless steel. Avoid using plastic for eating or cooking.

- ⑥ Cook with stainless steel, glass, cast iron, or clay. Avoid non-stick surfaces or cooking directly on aluminum. Food will taste much better when prepared with a higher quality vessel.

- ⑥ Consider induction for your next cooking appliance. It is easy to control the cooking process and energy efficient. I found it requires some practice and getting used to.

- ⑥ Choose a pot or pan large enough to handle the food but not so big that it is inefficient. The optimal size burner and pot provide more predictable results.

∽

DAIRY

- ⑥ Minimize significantly fermented products and eliminate aged products. Freshly made yogurt and buttermilk contain bacteria similar to the human digestive tract; small amounts, 1/2 cup or less, are recommended at room temperature. They are also nice as soups with spices and vegetables.

- ⑥ Eat dairy in small quantities, at room temperature or cooked.

- ⑥ Raw dairy is much easier to digest than processed. Enjoy it whenever possible (at room temperature or warm and in small quantities).

∽

FOOD AND TRAVEL

◍ Make up a rehydration drink to take on long plane flights; see the recipe in "Illness Recovery and Prevention." It may also be concentrated in a 3 ounce bottle to take on long trips. Revive your system with this hydrating beverage just before and after air, car, boat, or train travel.

◍ Prepare food to take on longer trips such as sweet potatoes, dosa, or grains with nuts and veggies.

◍ Hydrate yourself beforehand and drink water during the trip.

∽

FOOD CONSUMPTION

◍ Do not eat while cooking: no tasting or snacking. Having little bits before the meal initiates your digestion. Trust the cooking process and use intuition. There is no need to taste before serving.

◍ Be sure to consume the juice produced from cooking food. The liquid has much of the nutrients.

◍ Incorporate all six tastes (sweet, salty, sour, bitter, pungent, astringent) in each meal. Use spices to balance the tastes and to aid digestion.

◍ In small or moderate amounts, all of the tastes render balancing effects. In excess, they cause imbalance. An example is garlic. Used in moderation, it can be a purifier, whereas liberal use causes irritation of the digestive tract and over-activity of the mind. Moderate usage is 1-2 thin slices per serving.

⑥ Eat at regular meal times. Enjoy the heavier meal midday, followed by a lighter meal early in the evening.

⑥ Soak or cook raw nuts before eating. Minimize eating roasted nuts, as the *prana* is reduced in the roasting process and they are more difficult to digest. Be sure to chew nuts thoroughly or they will disturb the digestion.

⑥ Like attracts like and the opposite brings balance. For example, if you tend toward impatience or a hot temper, you may love chili peppers. Hot, spicy foods like these will take your *pitta* further out of balance. Another common example: craving light, airy, crunchy foods when you feel ungrounded and scattered. These foods will accentuate the *vata* imbalance. Choose spices and foods that you know will nourish you, rather than giving in to what you crave. Keep everything in moderation.

⑥ See *Freedom in Your Relationship with Food* or halepule.com for suggestions of types of grains, veggies, and legumes best suited for each constitution.

⑥ One-dish meals are comforting, especially for *vata dosha*. Prepare them with ingredients that are more augmenting than extractive to keep *vata* calm.

⑥ Avoid consuming a large quantity of water before a meal or any right after a meal as it dilutes the digestive juices. You may sip up to ½ cup of room temperature water with your meal to aid digestion.

⑥ Once you consume a snack, substantive drink, or light meal the body moves into the digestive process. Be sure to leave enough time for that digestion before eating or drinking again. Remember, eating again before the previous meal has digested disturbs digestion. Ongoing disturbance leads to bigger problems.

❦

FOOD PREPARATION

⑥ Choose meals from the recipes in this book and plan around available ingredients.

⑥ Cooking your food gently makes it accessible to your body and consciousness. While some people can eat raw food without experiencing negative consequences, most do not have strong enough digestive fire to handle it.

⑥ Cook with lids on pots and pans for energy efficiency, and to maintain moisture in the food. Legumes are an exception: bring them to a boil without the lid to reduce the gassiness. Continue cooking with lid.

⑥ Soaking grains, legumes, and nuts wakes up the *prana* and reduces cooking time.

⑥ If you live in a cold environment, warm the water a bit before adding to cooking vegetables.

⑥ Use herbal tea in place of water for cooking.

⑥ Consider the qualities and tastes combined with each dish.

⑥ The attitude of the cook goes into the food and then into those who consume it. Do not cook when feeling angry or resentful.

⑥ Let food sit for a few minutes after cooking, allowing the *prana* to settle. Serve it warm or at room temperature. Do not serve food cold. Cold food and drinks weaken the digestive fire.

∾

FOOD QUALITY AND SOURCING

⑥ Buy organic, biodynamic, or at least unsprayed food whenever possible for the good health of all beings and the planet. If you don't know the source of veggies, then peel and wash them very well. Fruits and vegetables with thin skin or seeds on the outside-- strawberries and tomatoes, for example--are best avoided if you suspect chemicals were used in the growing process.

⑥ Eat locally grown foods as much as possible to support your community's farmers, and to be in concert with nature.

⑥ Eat fruits and vegetables that are in season where you live. For example, fruit is cooling and best in the summer. If you live in a colder climate, some winter fruits such as cooked apples or pears may work well. Avoid tropical fruits in the winter unless you live in the tropics.

๖ Refined foods are any products that have been processed resulting in a loss of the natural balance. Most foods in packages fall into this category. Anytime the natural state of a food is altered, digestion is impaired. Biochemical changes from refinement interfere with natural digestion. As a result, toxins are created and the liver and other organs are required to do more work. Refined foods are extractive, rather than augmenting. For example, brown rice pasta is refined and the body is not able to make use of it the same as whole grain brown rice.

๖ Do not use tap water for cooking; it contains chlorine that is toxic for human and animal consumption. Filter or let it sit in sunlight for a couple of hours before using.

๖ Asafoetida (also called hing) is a spice used as a digestive aid and for taste, especially for cooking legumes. Use it in very tiny amounts. Its strength will vary according to the source. Buy online, in an Indian grocery store, or in the local health food store. Avoid asafoetida with chemical preservatives.

๖ Sea vegetables add the salt taste to cooking. They are full of minerals and nutrients that the body easily absorbs. Many kinds are available such as arame, hijiki, kombu, wakame, dulse, sea lettuce, nori, and others. Use sea vegetables acquired with sustainable practices and from the nearest ocean. Cook small amounts in legumes, veggies, or grains. Do not overuse them: 3-4 times a week is enough.

๖ Buy grains and legumes in bulk for better prices and convenience. Keep in airtight containers in a cool, dark location.

⑥ Be sure to buy split mung beans that are pale yellow or light green in color. Bright colors indicate toxic artificial coloring. Organic mung is available online from a number of sources if not found in the local health food store.

⑥ A common misconception is that Indian food is based in Ayurveda. This is not the case. Ayurveda may have originated in India, but few of today's popular Indian dishes follow the ancient principles.

⑥ Learning to recognize the qualities in foods comes with practice. As you become familiar with the various qualities it will become easier to know what is best for your constitution. For example, recognizing the heating or cooling quality in a food and how it affects you.

⑥ Learn to use your hands to feel the *prana* in food. Rub your hands together gently and bring them close to the food. You can feel the life force as tingling, pressure, warmth, or many other sensations. If you don't sense anything, then don't eat it, no matter how good it may look.

∽

FRUITS AND VEGETABLES

⑥ Fruits and veggies fresh from the earth brim with *prana*, or life force.

⑥ Sprouts are very light increasing *vata*. They will aggravate *vata* in large amounts. Clover and sunflower sprouts are the easiest to digest. Place them on top of cooking veggies for a few seconds at the end of the cooking process.

ⓖ Eat fruits alone. Do not mix fruit and vegetables in juice or whole form. Some say carrots and apples are an exception. Try it; if you experience any bloating or intestinal spasm afterward then it may not be a good idea.

ⓖ Keep citrus away from carbohydrates such as grains. Citrus is said to stop ptyalin, an enzyme produced in the mouth, from breaking down carbohydrates.

ⓖ Do not eat bananas with milk as they will curdle in the digestive tract causing fermentation and gas.

ⓖ Use lemon and lime in small amounts on occasion. More is not better. Overuse results in too much sourness, followed by acidity in the digestive tract.

⁓

GHEE

ⓖ Ghee is an ancient and *sattvic* food. Ideal for cooking, it does not burn unless heated excessively. It blends with other food nutrients to strengthen agni and nourish the body. See halepule.com for video and written instructions to prepare ghee.

ⓖ Do not use salted or commercial butter when making ghee. Although you can find ghee at your local health food store, you might find it more rewarding and less expensive to make at home. It is kept in the refrigerated section in stores by law, but should be kept at room temperature in a cupboard at home. Be careful not to contaminate it with wet utensils, food, or dirty fingers. This will lead to mold.

⑥ Ghee is good for all *doshas* in moderation. For those with excess *kapha*, minimal use is recommended. In recipes, use plenty of ghee when cooking for a person with symptoms of aggravated *vata* or *pitta*.

⑥ Use ghee as you would normally use butter or any oil. The taste may seem unusual at first—maybe a distant cousin of butter. Your palate quickly adjusts, and soon you forget why you ever found butter interesting!

⑥ In appropriate amounts, ghee does not exacerbate issues with cholesterol and will take care of omega 3 needs.

⑥ Ghee becomes liquid at about 72 degrees.

⑥ Heat ghee at a medium temperature, and then reduce heat to simmer spices. How long this takes will depend on the pan, room temperature, and type of burner.

∽

KITCHEN ORGANIZATION

⑥ Stock the kitchen pantry on a regular basis so the necessary ingredients are available for cooking.

⑥ Keep your kitchen orderly so that it is easy to find the necessary tools. Put things back in the same place after use.

⑥ Shop for fresh ingredients at least weekly. Keep at least 2 to 4 weeks of dried grains and legumes on hand for more efficient shopping and convenience.

◉ Plan the next day's meals the night before. Soak legumes or grains as needed.

◉ Take out all ingredients for food preparation before starting and clean up as you go.

◉ Preparing meals as a group, with friends or family, reduces prep time and encourages community. Keep discussions on a positive note.

∽

OILS

◉ Consume high quality oil and ghee on a regular basis. The "oil is bad" fad shifted the modern diet towards dry food, which lacks adequate oil and moisture. The result has been a serious loss of lubrication in the body and mind.

◉ All oils contain some degree of warming or cooling qualities. For example, sesame oil is warming and coconut oil is cooling. Almond oil is slightly warming and sunflower oil is neutral to warming.

◉ Black sesame oil has additional minerals and nutrients beyond the light sesame oil. Both are good.

∽

PRESSURE COOKING

⑥ Use a pressure cooker to reduce cooking time on grains and legumes. Get to know how to maintain pressure with the lowest level of heat. This will vary according to the cooktop as well as how much is in the pot.

⑥ Cook times shown in these recipes for a pressure cooker are for cooking once *at pressure*.

❧

SERVING SIZES

⑥ Adjust recipes using the following guidelines: for a hearty appetite, prepare ⅓–½ cup uncooked grain per person and for a more modest appetite ¼ cup uncooked grain. For legumes, the hearty appetite is ¼ cup dry and slightly less for a modest appetite. Vegetables will vary a bit by type, but it will be somewhere between ½ and 1 cup of augmenting veggies and ⅓-1 cup extractive per person. Remember to follow the balance between augmenting and extractive ingredients (60% / 40%) to promote peace and harmony in the body and mind.

❧

SPICES

⑥ Local spices and herbs such as basil, cilantro, parsley, and others can be used successfully as digestive aids and for balancing food preparation.

⑥ If cooking with spices is a new adventure for you, start with fresh ginger and cumin seeds. Be sure to use enough spices and allow them to cook long enough for their aromas to wake up. If the spices seem too weak, add a little more next time. The strength of spices is affected by their age, storage conditions, and the weather during their growing time.

⑥ Use fresh spices, dried seeds, and powder. Fresh herbs and seeds will tend to provide a fuller taste. A combination can work well, too. Some spices change characteristics with drying. Fresh ginger is balancing for all *doshas* in moderate amounts. Dried ginger, ground to powder, is more heating. Use it moderately and not at all when cooking for those with excess *pitta*.

⑥ Store spices and herbs out of daylight in a dark, cool cupboard. Use them up in six months. Compost or throw out old spices.

⑥ Keep fresh ginger and turmeric in a covered bowl of water in the refrigerator or on the counter for near term use.

⑥ Grind black pepper or other spices right before using for enhanced *prana* and taste. Use a coffee grinder or mortar and pestle.

⑥ Be flexible in the cooking process. Experiment with combining all ingredients in a pot versus simmering the spices in ghee/oil first. Note the difference and choose accordingly.

ILLNESS RECOVERY AND
PREVENTION

Ayurvedic texts suggest that life is a divine gift. Longevity allows us to thoroughly enjoy that gift. Ayurveda explores how to live fully while preventing disease. Diet and lifestyle (including attitude) are primary components in disease prevention, both of which you have control over.

Prevention requires respecting small messages from the body and mind. These messages, or symptoms, indicate when something is not right on the inside. The science of Ayurveda connects what you are doing to the results you are experiencing. How and what you eat, and the condition of your digestion, determine how easily you can prevent and recover from illness.

Illness and disease give many warnings before manifesting in ways that demand attention. Ayurveda looks at disease in six stages. Illness is much easier to reverse when recognized at an early stage. By the time problems show up in laboratory tests, a disease has progressed at least to the fourth stage, but is still reversible with changes in attitude, diet, and lifestyle. Tune into smaller symptoms, and make changes to eliminate them, to divert more serious problems.

ADDRESSING IMBALANCES

Be open to recognizing when life is out of balance. Symptoms such as fatigue, colds, headaches, dizziness, and physical and mental tension are signs of imbalance. If your immune system is not weak, you will not get the cold that is going around. Once you realize the status of your well-being and become willing to make changes, you will be pointed in the right direction for improvement. Make it a priority to feel well, balanced, and harmonious, and improvement will come.

Take steps toward well-being by adjusting your habits around food, eating, and lifestyle. Well-being is not just about eating the "right" food. The "right" food may not be right for you. Eating food that someone says is a good food without considering your own constitution is an external fix that may have limited effect.

Adjusting your attitude changes your thinking and behavior. Your attitude dictates your energy and hence, your ability to digest life and food. When you harbor feelings of anger, fear, resentment, and lack of acceptance, your digestion will be disturbed. Ongoing disturbance becomes a breeding ground for illness and disease.

When your body sends you a message through a symptom, it is time to do something different. Continuing the same behaviors brings more of the same results. Make a shift in your thinking. Recognize that life is a process and that you are enough. Acceptance of where you are will facilitate a change toward balance.

When you do not feel well, no matter what the symptom, eat food that is easily digested. It gives you, your body, and *agni* the maximum opportunity to recover quickly.

∽

SYMPTOMS AND CAUSES OF INDIGESTION AND FERMENTATION

Symptoms of Indigestion and Fermentation Include:

- Weakness
- Diarrhea
- Illness
- Gassiness
- Heaviness
- Belching and burping
- Acid reflux
- Bloating
- Headache
- Stuffy nose
- Mucous
- Feeling sleepy or the need to lay down
- Feeling groggy upon awakening

Causes of Indigestion and Fermentation Include:

- Overindulgence
- Eating too fast
- Not chewing enough
- Going to sleep while still digesting food
- Laying down after eating
- Eating again on top of undigested food
- Eating too often
- Not allowing digestion to rejuvenate
- Poor food combinations

- Eating cold foods or drinks
- Overeating at one sitting
- Too much dense and dry food
- Too much liquid during and soon after meals
- Negative attitudes and disturbed emotional states

- Nervousness
- Anger
- Irritation
- Fear
- Resistance
- Worry
- Anxiety
- Excitement

∽

REJUVENATING DIGESTIVE FIRE (AGNI)

If your digestive fire, or *agni,* has been compromised, rejuvenate by changing your attitude and eating habits. The meals and recipes listed below easily supply nutrients to the body tissues while your *agni* repairs itself. **Rest,** possibly skip a meal to allow *agni* to recover strength, and then eat simple foods, such as the soupy rice variations described here. Remember, the strength of your *agni* relates to your attitude and degree of acceptance as much as your physical actions.

∽

RECIPES FOR ILLNESS RECOVERY AND PREVENTION

Soupy rice variations for illness recovery and prevention
serves 4 | preparation time: 15-20 minutes; 25-35 minutes for kitchadi | *Augmenting*

These rice variations are a progression of increasing consistency that allows the digestive fire to recover. Except for kitchadi, cook other versions for approximately 15-18 minutes. The Sanskrit name for each progression (derived from ancient Ayurvedic texts) is given in parentheses. These variations are also sometimes referred to as kanyi or kunyi.

- 1 cup white basmati rice to 6 cups water (manda), pinch mineral salt, pinch of ghee, pinch of jaggery, sucanat, or raw sugar. Cook ingredients until rice is soft. A thin rice liquid.

- 1 cup white basmati rice to 4 cups water (peya), pinch mineral salt, pinch of ghee, pinch of jaggery, sucanat, or raw sugar. Cook ingredients until rice is soft. A thicker rice liquid.

- 1 cup white basmati rice to 2 cups water (vilepi), pinch mineral salt, pinch of ghee, pinch of jaggery, sucanat, or raw sugar. Cook ingredients until rice is soft. A mushy rice soup.

- ¾ cup white basmati rice, ¼ cup split mung beans to 2-4 cups water (yusha), ¼ tsp mineral salt, ½ tsp of ghee, ½ tsp fresh grated ginger. Cook ingredients until soft. May also add small amount cooked vegetables. A thicker rice soup.

- 1 cup white basmati rice, 1½ cups water (odana), ½ tsp mineral salt, 1 tsp ghee, ½ tsp fresh grated ginger, ½-1 tsp fresh ground turmeric. Cook ingredients until rice is soft. An easily digested cooked rice.

⊚ ¾ cup white basmati rice, ¼-⅓ cup split mung beans to 6 cups water (kitchadi), ½ tsp mineral salt, 1-2 Tbsp ghee, 1 Tbsp fresh grated ginger, 1 tsp cumin seeds, 1 tsp coriander seeds, 1 tsp brown mustard seeds, ⅓ tsp asafoetida, 1 tsp cardamom powder, 3-4 cups chopped veggies such as squash, pumpkin, beets, and/or kale. Simmer the seeds and spices in ghee until the spices' aroma comes up. Add the rice and split mung, stirring together for 1-2 minutes. Add the water and simmer for 20-30 minutes. Add vegetables (optional) and finish cooking. Kitchadi is easily digested, nutrient rich and excellent for gentle cleansing as well as illness recovery.

Kambalika

serves 4 | preparation time: 10 minutes | *Augmenting*

- ¼ tsp fresh grated ginger
- ¼ tsp cumin seeds
- ¼ tsp mustard seeds
- ⅓ tsp powdered asafoetida
- 1 Tbsp ground split mung beans
- 1 Tbsp ghee
- 1 cup fresh buttermilk
- ½ cup water
- 1-2 Tbsp fresh chopped mint

Sauté ginger, cumin seeds, mustard seeds, asafoetida, and split mung in ghee. Warm the buttermilk with water, adding ghee and spices. Garnish with mint.

Tips: Kambalika helps build *agni* and brings balance to intestinal flora. Enjoy it twice each week. A small amount of cooked vegetables may be added.

Rehydration drink

serves 1 | preparation time: 5 minutes | *Augmenting*

- ⑥ 2 cups water
- ⑥ 1 Tbsp honey
- ⑥ ¼ tsp mineral salt
- ⑥ 10 drops fresh lime or lemon juice

Warm ½ cup water and pour over honey and salt dissolving both into the water. Add the remaining water and lime. Stir and drink ½ cup at a time.

Tip: Revive yourself with this drink after a day in the sun, before and after airline and auto travel, or anytime you are exposed to dry air such as central heating and air conditioning.

Digestive aid-as-appetizer

serves 1 | preparation time: 3 minutes | *Augmenting*

- ⑥ pinch mineral salt
- ⑥ 2-3 drops lime
- ⑥ ¼ tsp fresh grated ginger

Add salt and lime to ginger. Chew well 10-15 minutes before eating. This appetizer prepares the body for the meal to come. Fresh ginger is balancing for all *doshas* and stimulates the beginning of the digestive process. In general, food appetizers are not recommended. Eating small amounts in advance of a meal confuses the body and disturbs digestion.

OTHER DIGESTIVE AIDS

- ⑥ If you find you experience gas or bloating after eating a meal, chew ½ tsp ginger with 3-5 drops lime thoroughly for quick relief.

- ⑥ Chew fennel seed after a meal to aid digestion.

- ⑥ Make a tasty concoction of fennel seeds, maple syrup, mineral salt, fresh ginger, fresh or powdered turmeric, rose petals, and fresh ground black pepper. Combine and chew 1 tsp 10 minutes before or just after meals.

༄

DAY OF FASTING

A day of fasting provides a rest for your digestive tract. It allows *agni* to recover so that what you eat afterward will be digested and utilized. Fasting beyond one day should be under the guidance of an experienced practitioner. It is most effective with prayer and meditation throughout the day.

- ⑥ For keeping *vata* calm, drink warm liquids such as rice water, veggie broth, and herbal teas.

- ⑥ For *pitta*, drink grape or apricot juice diluted ½ with water or coconut water.

- ⑥ For kapha, fast with room temperature or warm water, or vegetable broth.

BREAKFAST

B reakfast is meant to break the fast that takes place through the night. Be easy on your digestion at breakfast to maintain a strong *agni* throughout the day.

- ☉ Cook your grains with nuts, raisins, or apples for a great start to your day. For easiest digestion do not combine the nuts with raisins or apples. Soaking raisins overnight in a small amount of water and adding both to the cooked grain works well also.

- ☉ Ayurveda does not recommend mixing grains with milk, banana, eggs, or dates. The heaviness of these foods taxes *agni* and slows digestion, resulting in fermentation and gas in the digestive tract.

- ☉ Sometimes it may be appropriate to eat only fresh fruit or a simple fruit smoothie (see "Light Meals, Sides, and Drinks"). Include no more than three different fruits, as too much variation is difficult for digestion.

- ☉ Use easily digested, augmenting foods, like sweet potatoes or squash, as another alternative. Dosas provide additional protein for more substantive needs at breakfast. See "Light Meals, Sides, and Drinks" for a dosa recipe.

Here are some suggestions for breakfast. Experiment and see what works best for you. How you feel 1 hour, 4 hours, and 12-24 hours later tells the story of what happened with the food.

∾

BREAKFAST RECIPES

Cooked apples with raisins

serves 4 | preparation time: <10 minutes | *Augmenting*

- ⑥ 2 chopped apples
- ⑥ ½ cup raisins
- ⑥ water
- ⑥ 1 tsp cinnamon powder
- ⑥ 1 Tbsp ghee

Combine all ingredients in pot with water ½ the level of apples. Add cinnamon and ghee. Simmer until knife goes in easily.

Tips: Serve with breakfast grain or individually. Be sure to consume the juice as well as the apples for maximum taste and nutrients. You can also cook ½-1 tsp of chopped ginger in the ghee prior to adding the rest of the ingredients.

Cooked bananas

serves 4 | preparation time: <10 minutes | *Augmenting*

- ෴ 2 Tbsp ghee or 1 Tbsp ghee and 1 Tbsp coconut oil
- ෴ 4 medium size ripe bananas sliced lengthwise
- ෴ 1/4 tsp each cinnamon and cardamom powder

Heat ghee with spices and simmer banana for 3-5 minutes. Add a dusting of clove powder or nutmeg for additional warmth.

Tips: Sometimes extra ghee is necessary, depending on how ripe the bananas are. An especially ripe banana needs less ghee.

Myraji's sunrise delight

serves 4 | preparation time: 20 minutes | *Augmenting*

- 2 cups white basmati rice
- 5 cups water
- 2 Tbsp ghee
- ¾-1 tsp mineral salt
- 1 tsp cinnamon powder
- ⅓ tsp ginger powder
- 1 cup raisins
- ½ cup chopped apricots

Combine all ingredients in pot. Bring to boil with lid on and turn to simmer for 15 minutes, until soupy in consistency. For an even soupier grain, add more water or an herbal tea. The dried fruit will soak up some of the water.

Pancakes

serves 4 | preparation time: 15-20 minutes |
Augmenting

- ⚇ 2 cups freshly ground flour
- ⚇ ½ cup rice milk or soy or almond milk
- ⚇ ½ tsp cinnamon powder
- ⚇ ½ tsp cumin powder
- ⚇ ½ tsp coriander powder
- ⚇ 1-2 Tbsp ghee or sesame oil

Mix ingredients gently to make a batter, not dough. It should be thick, not runny. Cook first side until bubbles form then turn to other side. Top with maple syrup or a little yogurt and honey.

Tips: Shred ½-1 cup carrots or 1-2 Tbsp ground split mung beans into the batter. Mix 2 tsp honey and 1 tsp tahini for an excellent topping. Add applesauce or cooked apples to the batter for more moisture and sweet taste. Remember- it is recommended to consume fruit separately from other foods such as vegetables, beans, and dairy.

Rice and whole wheat or barley and whole wheat are excellent flour combinations.

Quinoa with apples

serves 4 | preparation time: 20 minutes | *Augmenting*

- ⑥ 1 ½ cups quinoa
- ⑥ 4 cups water
- ⑥ 1 Tbsp ghee
- ⑥ ½-1 tsp mineral salt
- ⑥ 1, 3-inch cinnamon stick
- ⑥ ¾ tsp coriander powder
- ⑥ 1-2 cups chopped apples

Combine quinoa, ghee, salt, cinnamon, coriander, and chopped apples. Bring to a boil, cover with a lid, and reduce to simmer for 10-15 minutes.

Tips: Always rinse quinoa prior to cooking as it is covered in an indigestible powder. Use other grains such as barley, rice, bulgur, or millet. Try varying the spices. For a savory flavor, use cumin, coriander, and black pepper.

Spiced wild rice

serves 4 | preparation time: 45-50 minutes; with pressure cooker, 20 minutes | *Augmenting*

- ⑥ 2 cups wild rice
- ⑥ 4 ½ cups water
- ⑥ 2 Tbsp ghee
- ⑥ ¾ tsp mineral salt
- ⑥ 1 tsp fresh chopped ginger
- ⑥ 1 ½ tsp coriander powder
- ⑥ ¼ tsp powdered turmeric
- ⑥ 1 tsp cinnamon powder

Combine ingredients in a pot. Bring to a boil and then simmer 45 minutes, or cook 18 minutes at pressure. When finished, stir and let sit for 3-5 minutes.

Tips: Add 1-2 Tbsp ground split mung beans for a heartier breakfast. For a different flavor experience, cook your spices in ghee first until the aroma comes up, and then add rice and water.

Vegetable grain breakfast

serves 4 | preparation time: 40 minutes; with pressure cooker, 18 minutes | *Augmenting*

- ⑥ 1 ½ cups grain
- ⑥ 4 cups water
- ⑥ 1-2 Tbsp ghee
- ⑥ ½-1 tsp mineral salt

Combine ingredients in a pot. Bring to a boil and then simmer for a length of time appropriate for the grain chosen. With a pressure cooker, the cook time is reduced again.

Tips: Choose any of the grains, including rice, steel cut oats, barley, millet, quinoa, or bulgur. Soak the grains overnight to reduce the cooking time. Use soak water for cooking. Vary the spices according to how you feel that day. Add chopped nuts such as cashew or pecans at the beginning of cooking. Add shredded carrot or beet and chopped cilantro at the end of cooking for a wonderful dish. Cook in a 1:3 or 1:4 grain to water ratio, depending on how thick or thin you like it. Grinding the grains and then cooking the grain meal will make a mushy, creamy texture. Try it with rice or bulgur. This variation is particularly good when recovering from illness. The nutrients are readily available to the body and easily digested.

GRAINS

Grains, such as rice, quinoa, and bulgur, are grounding and augmenting. Whole grains are digestible and enjoyable, providing nourishment and nurturing.

Grains that are refined into pasta become extractive, and are not particularly nourishing. Many people erroneously lump all carbohydrates in the same category. Refined carbohydrates leave you craving more food to feel nourished. Hence, part of the reason so many people have trouble with "carbs."

Stay with whole grains as much as possible. Cook them well and chew them well. Notice the difference in how you feel. (Remember not to eat past the first belch.)

Here are some tips in preparing and consuming grains:

- Some whole grains can be soaked 2-8 hours in advance of cooking to reduce the cooking time. Use the soak water for cooking.

- Do not add salt until it is time to cook the grain.

- White rice, such as basmati or jasmine, does not need to be soaked. Neither does quinoa.

- If cooking conventionally, boil and cook grains with the lid on so that the grain absorbs the moisture.

- Bulgur is fluffier if soaked before cooking. It may be eaten raw after a few hours of soaking by those with strong digestion.

⑥ Cook times for conventional cooking are estimates and will vary according to the type of rice, pot, cooktop, and temperature/humidity in the environment; make sure most of the water is absorbed.

⑥ If *vata dosha* is aggravated or constipation is present, then avoid millet. If your *vata* seems balanced, then the millet recipe may work well. Enjoy it once or twice a month with plenty of ghee and see how you feel afterward.

∿

GRAIN RECIPES

Barley

serves 4 | preparation time: 40-45 minutes; with pressure cooker, 20 minutes | *Augmenting*

⑥ 1 ½ cups barley

⑥ 3 cups water

⑥ 1-2 Tbsp ghee

⑥ ¾ tsp mineral salt

Combine all ingredients in pot, bring to a boil, and reduce to simmer for 35-40 minutes, or cook 18 minutes at pressure.

Tip: Reduce cooking time by 5-10 minutes by soaking the barley at least 2 hours in advance.

Barley with saffron

serves 4 | preparation time: 35-40 minutes; with pressure cooker, 15 minutes | *Augmenting*

- ✆ 2 cups pearl barley
- ✆ 3 cups water
- ✆ 1 Tbsp coconut oil
- ✆ ¾ tsp mineral salt
- ✆ 5-10 strands saffron

Combine barley, water, coconut oil, and mineral salt in pot. Bring to a boil and reduce to simmer for 30-35 minutes. Stir in saffron toward end. For pressure cooker, combine barley, water, oil and salt, bring to pressure and cook for 15 minutes. Stir in saffron after pressure drops.

Tip: Reduce cooking time by 5-10 minutes by soaking the barley at least 2 hours in advance.

Brown and wild rice mix

serves 4 | preparation time: 45-50 minutes; with pressure cooker, 20 minutes | *Augmenting*

- ⑥ 1 ½ cups brown and wild rice mix
- ⑥ 1 Tbsp ghee
- ⑥ ½ tsp mineral salt
- ⑥ 3 cups water

Combine all ingredients in pot, bring to a boil, and reduce to simmer for 45 minutes, or cook 18 minutes at pressure.

Tips: Reduce cooking time by 5-10 minutes by soaking the rice at least 2 hours in advance.

Brown basmati rice

serves 4 | preparation time: 35-40 minutes; with pressure cooker, 18 minutes | *Augmenting*

- ⑤ 2 cups brown basmati rice
- ⑤ 3 cups water
- ⑤ 1 Tbsp ghee
- ⑤ ¾ tsp mineral salt

Combine all ingredients in pot, bring to a boil, and reduce to simmer for 35 minutes, or cook 15 minutes at pressure.

Tip: Reduce cooking time by 5-10 minutes by soaking the rice at least 2 hours in advance.

Brown basmati rice with saffron

serves 4 | preparation time: 35-40 minutes; with pressure cooker, 20 minutes | *Augmenting*

- ⑥ 2 cups brown basmati rice
- ⑥ 3 cups water
- ⑥ 1 Tbsp ghee
- ⑥ ¾ tsp mineral salt
- ⑥ 5-10 strands saffron

Combine rice, water, ghee, and mineral salt in pot. Bring to a boil and reduce to simmer for 35 minutes. Stir in saffron toward end. For pressure cooker, combine rice, water, and salt, bring to pressure and cook for 15 minutes. Stir in ghee and saffron after pressure drops.

Tip: Saffron is effective at enhancing the effects of other spices and food. It supports the ready assimilation of nutrients into the tissues of the body. Reduce cooking time by 5-10 minutes by soaking the rice at least 2 hours in advance.

Bulgur wheat

serves 4 | preparation time: 20 minutes | *Augmenting*

- ⚕ 2 cups bulgur wheat
- ⚕ 4 cups water
- ⚕ 1 Tbsp ghee
- ⚕ ½ tsp mineral salt

Soak bulgur for 1 hour. Combine all ingredients in pot, bring to a boil, and reduce to simmer for 15 minutes. Reduce cooking time by 5-10 minutes by soaking the bulgur at least 2 hours in advance.

Tip: Bulgur may be soaked for 2-4 hours and can be eaten raw or just warmed slightly.

Bulgur wheat with sesame oil

serves 4 | preparation time: 20 minutes | *Augmenting*

- ◍ 2 cups bulgur wheat
- ◍ 4 cups water
- ◍ 1 Tbsp sesame oil
- ◍ ¾ tsp mineral salt

Soak bulgur for 1 hour. Combine all ingredients in pot, bring to a boil, and reduce to simmer for 15 minutes.

Tip: Reduce cooking time by 5-10 minutes by soaking the bulgur at least 2 hours in advance.

Millet

serves 4 | preparation time: 35-45 minutes; with pressure cooker, 18 minutes | *Augmenting*

- ۞ 1 ¾ cups millet
- ۞ 3 ½ cups water (or exchange herbal tea for water)
- ۞ 2 Tbsp ghee
- ۞ 1 tsp mineral salt

Combine all ingredients in pot, bring to a boil, and reduce to simmer for 35-40 minutes, or cook 15 minutes at pressure.

Tip: Reduce cooking time by 5-10 minutes by soaking the millet at least 2 hours in advance.

Millet with ginger

serves 4 | preparation time: 35-45 minutes; with pressure cooker, 18 minutes | *Augmenting*

- ⊙ 1 ¾ cups millet
- ⊙ 3 ½ cups water
- ⊙ 2 Tbsp ghee
- ⊙ ½ tsp fresh grated ginger
- ⊙ 1 tsp mineral salt
- ⊙ ½ tsp fresh ground black pepper
- ⊙ ¼ tsp ground cinnamon

Combine millet, water, salt, and 1 Tbsp ghee in pot, bring to a boil, and reduce to simmer for 35-40 minutes, or cook 15 minutes at pressure. In a separate pan, heat remaining ghee, add spices, and cook until the spices' aroma comes up. Add to millet once cooked.

Tip: Reduce cooking time by 5-10 minutes by soaking the millet at least 2 hours in advance.

Quinoa with ghee

serves 4 | preparation time: 20 minutes | *Augmenting*

- ⚕ 2 cups quinoa
- ⚕ 4 cups water
- ⚕ 1-2 Tbsp ghee
- ⚕ ¾ tsp mineral salt

Rinse grain thoroughly with clean water and place in pot. Add water, ghee, and mineral salt. Bring to a boil and reduce to simmer for 15-20 minutes.

Quinoa with pistachio

serves 4 | preparation time: 20 minutes | *Augmenting*

- ⑥ 1 ½ cup quinoa
- ⑥ 2 ¾ cups water
- ⑥ 1 Tbsp coconut oil
- ⑥ 1 Tbsp urud dhal
- ⑥ ½ tsp mineral salt
- ⑥ 1 handful of coarsely chopped pistachio nuts

Combine quinoa, water, oil, dhal, and mineral salt in pot. Bring to a boil and reduce to simmer for 15-20 minutes. Add pistachio 5 minutes before grain is finished cooking.

Quinoa with turmeric

serves 4 | preparation time: 20 minutes | *Extractive*

- ֍ 1 ½ cups quinoa
- ֍ 3 cups water
- ֍ 1 Tbsp ghee
- ֍ ½ tsp fresh grated or powdered turmeric
- ֍ ½ tsp mineral salt

Combine quinoa, water, ghee, and mineral salt. Bring to a boil and reduce to simmer for 15-20 minutes.

Tip: Serve separately, or combine quinoa into complementary soup.

Spicy rice

serves 4 | preparation time: 20 minutes; with pressure cooker, 15 minutes | *Augmenting*

- ⊚ 2 cups white basmati rice
- ⊚ ½ tsp mineral salt
- ⊚ 3 cups water
- ⊚ 2 Tbsp ghee
- ⊚ 1 tsp fresh grated ginger
- ⊚ 1 tsp fresh grated turmeric
- ⊚ 1 tsp cumin seeds
- ⊚ 1 tsp coriander seeds
- ⊚ 12 black peppercorns
- ⊚ ¼ tsp cinnamon powder
- ⊚ ¼ cup fresh chopped cilantro

Combine rice, mineral salt, and water in pot. Bring to a boil and simmer for 15-18 minutes, or cook 10 minutes at pressure. In a separate pan, heat the ghee and simmer ginger, turmeric, cumin, coriander, peppercorns, and cinnamon powder until the spices' aroma comes up. Pour on cooked rice and top with fresh cilantro.

Sushi rice

serves 4 | preparation time: 20 minutes for white basmati rice, 35-40 minutes for brown rice; with pressure cooker, 10-15 minutes for white basmati rice, 18 minutes for brown rice | *Augmenting*

- ⑥ 2 cups basmati rice (white or brown)
- ⑥ 3 cups water
- ⑥ ¾ tsp mineral salt
- ⑥ Few drops ume plum vinegar (optional)

Combine all ingredients in pot, bring to a boil, and reduce to simmer for 18 minutes for white rice and 30 minutes for brown rice. For pressure cooker, cook 10 minutes for white rice and 20 minutes for brown rice.

Tip: To achieve a sticky effect, add a little extra water or a few drops of ume plum vinegar.

White basmati rice

serves 4 | preparation time: 20 minutes; with pressure cooker, 15 minutes | *Augmenting*

- ꙮ 2 cups white basmati rice
- ꙮ 3 cups water
- ꙮ 1 Tbsp ghee
- ꙮ ¾ tsp mineral salt

Combine all ingredients in pot, bring to a boil, and reduce to simmer for 15-18 minutes, or cook 10-12 minutes at pressure.

White basmati rice with teff

serves 4 | preparation time: 20 minutes; with pressure cooker, 12-15 minutes | *Augmenting*

- ⟲ 2 cups white basmati rice
- ⟲ 3 ½ cups water
- ⟲ ¼ cup teff
- ⟲ 1 Tbsp ghee
- ⟲ ¾ tsp mineral salt

Combine all ingredients in pot, bring to a boil, and reduce to simmer for 15-18 minutes, or cook 10-12 minutes at pressure.

Tip: Teff also combines nicely with barley, cooked in a similar manner as above.

White basmati rice with turmeric

serves 4 | preparation time: 15-20 minutes; with pressure cooker, 10-15 minutes | *Augmenting*

- ⚕ 1 ½ cups white basmati rice
- ⚕ 2 ¼ - 2 ½ cups water
- ⚕ 1 Tbsp ghee
- ⚕ ¾ tsp mineral salt
- ⚕ ½ tsp powdered turmeric

Combine all ingredients in pot, bring to a boil, and reduce to simmer for 15-17 minutes, or cook 10 minutes at pressure.

GRAINS

Wild rice

serves 4 | preparation time: 45-50 minutes; with pressure cooker, 25 minutes | *Augmenting*

- 1 ½ cups wild rice
- 1 Tbsp ghee
- 3 cups water
- ¾ tsp mineral salt

Combine all ingredients in pot, bring to a boil, and reduce to simmer for 45 minutes, or cook 20-22 minutes at pressure.

Tip: Reduce cooking time by 5-10 minutes by soaking the rice at least 2 hours in advance.

LEGUMES

Legumes are extractive and drying. Cook them with ghee, oil, mineral salt, spices, and water to assist in digestion and assimilation.

Here are some tips for preparing and consuming legumes:

- Most beans are more easily digested when soaked overnight or at least 4 hours in advance of cooking. Be sure to throw out the soak water and cook with fresh water. It is not necessary to soak lentils, and some of the smaller beans, such as adzukis and black-eyed peas, can be cooked in a pressure cooker without soaking.

- Preparation times in the recipes assume legumes have been soaked (where appropriate). If not soaked, depending upon the legume, add at least 10 minutes or more to conventional cooking time.

- Measurements in the recipes are for dried legumes.

- Recipe instructions in this book are for traditional stovetop cooking unless pressure-cooking is mentioned.

- If you like beans with more liquid then add more water at the beginning of the cooking process.

ⓖ Cook legumes until they are soft.

ⓖ Cook sea vegetables such as kombu with legumes to increase digestibility, thicken the juice, and add the salt taste. You may want to add a little extra water.

ⓖ Simmer spices in ghee or oil to wake them up before adding the legumes. Alternately, try cooking them all together. Both techniques work; see which one you prefer.

ⓖ Asafoetida is an excellent spice for making legumes easier to digest. It has a strong taste, so very small amounts are appropriate. Be careful when purchasing it; many companies put unwanted preservatives into the powder these days. Ask your local store buyer to stock some without preservatives.

ⓖ Because legumes are extractive, they will move out any fermented and undigested food lingering in the digestive tract from previous meals. This is why they sometimes seem to give you gas and other times not. In other words, the condition of the digestive tract is reflected by your response to the beans. (This assumes you eat a moderate amount of well-cooked beans.) With moderation and a balance between augmenting and extractive foods, most people can enjoy legumes comfortably.

⑥ If you prepare legumes and rice in the same pot, cook with the lid on to retain enough water in the cooking process.

⑥ Split mung beans are often called dhal. It is not necessary to soak them. Whole mung beans are also good, but more challenging to digest. These are best when soaked in advance. Visit the resource guide on my website at www.halepule. com/resourceguide for information on where to purchase split mung beans online.

⑥ *Vata*-aggravated individuals and those with a predominantly *vata* constitution should eat smaller amounts of legumes, emphasizing split mung beans as they are the easiest to digest.

LEGUME RECIPES

Adzuki and garbanzo hummus

serves 4 | preparation time: 45-50 minutes; with pressure cooker, 25 minutes | *Augmenting*

- ⑥ ½ cup adzuki beans
- ⑥ ½ cup garbanzo beans
- ⑥ ¾ tsp mineral salt
- ⑥ ¼ tsp asafoetida
- ⑥ 2-3 Tbsp sesame oil
- ⑥ 1 strip kombu cut in small pieces
- ⑥ water
- ⑥ 1 Tbsp tahini
- ⑥ 10 drops fresh lime juice

Combine beans, mineral salt, asafoetida, 1 Tbsp sesame oil, and kombu in pot. Add water to cover the beans by ⅓ inch and stir. Bring to a boil, reduce to simmer, and cover with a lid for 30-40 minutes, or cook 20 minutes at pressure. Combine cooled cooked beans and liquid in blender. Add 2 Tbsp sesame oil, tahini, lime, and a little water if needed for blending. Blend to a smooth consistency.

Adzuki beans

serves 4 | preparation time: 35-40 minutes; with pressure cooker, 15-20 minutes | *Extractive*

- ⑥ 1 cup adzuki beans
- ⑥ 1 Tbsp ghee or black sesame oil
- ⑥ 1-2 Tbsp leafy nori cut in small pieces
- ⑥ 2-4 bay leaves
- ⑥ ½ tsp mineral salt
- ⑥ ½ tsp powdered asafoetida
- ⑥ ¼ tsp powdered cinnamon
- ⑥ water

Combine all ingredients in pot. Add water to cover the beans by ⅓ inch and stir. Bring to a boil, reduce to simmer, and cover with a lid for 30-35 minutes, or cook 18 minutes at pressure.

Black eyed peas

serves 4 | preparation time: 30-35 minutes; with pressure cooker, 20 minutes | *Extractive*

- ⑥ 1 cup black eyed peas
- ⑥ 1-2 Tbsp ghee
- ⑥ 1 large strip kombu cut in small pieces
- ⑥ ¾ tsp mineral salt
- ⑥ ¼ tsp asafoetida powder
- ⑥ 1½ tsp cumin powder
- ⑥ water

Combine all ingredients in pot. Add water to cover the beans by ⅓ inch and stir. Bring to a boil, reduce to simmer, and cover with a lid for 25-30 minutes, or cook 15-18 minutes at pressure.

Black eyed peas and adzukis

serves 4 | preparation time: 45-50 minutes; with pressure cooker, 20-25 minutes | *Extractive*

- ⑥ ½ cup black eyed peas
- ⑥ ½ cup adzuki beans
- ⑥ ½ tsp mineral salt
- ⑥ ¼ tsp powdered asafoetida
- ⑥ 1 Tbsp ghee
- ⑥ 2 tsp cumin powder
- ⑥ ¼ tsp cinnamon powder
- ⑥ sprinkle fresh ground black pepper
- ⑥ ¼ cup arame
- ⑥ water

Combine all ingredients in pot. Add water to cover the beans by ⅓ inch and stir. Bring to a boil, reduce to simmer, and cover with a lid for 40-45 minutes, or cook 20 minutes at pressure.

Black eyed peas with black sesame oil

serves 4 | preparation time: 40-45 minutes; with pressure cooker, 20 minutes | *Extractive*

- ⑥ 1 cup black eyed peas
- ⑥ 1-2 Tbsp black sesame oil
- ⑥ ¾ tsp mineral salt
- ⑥ ¼ tsp powdered asafoetida
- ⑥ 1 Tbsp powdered cumin
- ⑥ 1 Tbsp powdered coriander
- ⑥ 1 tsp powdered cardamom
- ⑥ water

Combine all ingredients in pot. Add water to cover the beans by ⅓ inch and stir. Bring to a boil, reduce to simmer, and cover with a lid for 30-35 minutes, or cook 18 minutes at pressure.

Black lentils

serves 4 | preparation time: 30 minutes; with pressure cooker, 15-20 minutes | *Extractive*

- ⑤ 1 cup black lentils
- ⑤ 3 cups water
- ⑤ 1 Tbsp ghee
- ⑤ 1 Tbsp hijiki
- ⑤ ½ tsp mineral salt

Combine all ingredients in a pot, stir, and bring to a boil. Reduce to simmer and cover with a lid for 35-40 minutes, or cook 18 minutes at pressure.

When the shell is removed from black lentils it is called urud dhal. The color is then off white. Both black lentils and urud dhal are great as a one-quarter combination with another legume. They are particularly nutritive and assist in building vitality. On their own they can be heavy for someone with weaker digestion.

Brown lentils with arame

serves 4 | preparation time: 35-40 minutes; with pressure cooker, 20 minutes | *Extractive*

- ۞ 1-2 Tbsp ghee or sesame oil
- ۞ 1 tsp fresh grated ginger
- ۞ 1 tsp fresh grated turmeric
- ۞ 1-2 tsp brown mustard seed
- ۞ ½ tsp mineral salt
- ۞ ½ tsp fresh ground black pepper
- ۞ ¼ tsp asafoetida powder
- ۞ ½ tsp rosemary
- ۞ ¼ cup chopped basil
- ۞ ½ tsp cinnamon powder
- ۞ 1 cup brown lentils
- ۞ ¼-½ cup arame
- ۞ 3 ½ cups water

Heat ghee or oil on medium heat and add ginger, turmeric, mustard seed, salt, pepper, asafoetida, and rosemary. Cook until the spices' aroma comes up. Add basil and cinnamon and stir. Add brown lentils, arame, and water. Stir, bring to a boil, then reduce to simmer and cover with a lid until lentils are soft.

Tip: Serve with an augmenting grain or side such as chapati.

Dhal soup

serves 4 | preparation time: 30 minutes; with pressure cooker, 15 minutes | *Extractive*

- ⑥ 1-2 Tbsp ghee
- ⑥ 1-2 tsp fresh grated ginger
- ⑥ 1 tsp fresh grated turmeric
- ⑥ 1½ tsp cumin seeds
- ⑥ ¼ tsp asafoetida
- ⑥ 1 tsp mineral salt
- ⑥ small handful arame
- ⑥ 1 cup split mung beans
- ⑥ 4+ cups water

Heat ghee on medium heat and add spices and seasonings. Cook until the spices' aroma comes up. Add split mung and stir to coat with ghee and spices. Add the water, stir, and bring to a boil. Reduce to simmer and cover with a lid for 25 minutes, or cook 12-15 minutes at pressure.

Dhal soup with urud dhal

serves 4 | preparation time: 30-35 minutes; with pressure cooker, 20 minutes | *Extractive*

- ⑥ 1-2 Tbsp ghee
- ⑥ 1 tsp mineral salt
- ⑥ 1 tsp fresh grated ginger
- ⑥ ¼ tsp powdered asafoetida
- ⑥ 1 tsp hijiki
- ⑥ 1½ tsp cumin seeds
- ⑥ ½ tsp powdered turmeric
- ⑥ ¾ cup split mung beans
- ⑥ ½ cup urud dhal
- ⑥ 4-5 cups water

Heat ghee on medium heat and add spices. Cook until the spices' aroma comes up. Add split mung, urud dhal, water and stir. Bring to a boil, reduce to simmer, and cover with a lid for 25-30 minutes, or cook 18 minutes at pressure.

Tips: Urud dhal refers to black lentils with the shell removed and split, so they are small and whitish. Contributing to vitality, they are excellent in combination with other beans such as split mung. They are too heavy on their own. Adding more water will make a thinner soup; less water, and it can become like dumplings.

Dhal (thicker)

serves 4 | preparation time: 35-40 minutes; with pressure cooker, 15-18 minutes | *Extractive*

- ⚕ 1-2 Tbsp ghee
- ⚕ 1 tsp mineral salt
- ⚕ 1+ tsp cumin seeds
- ⚕ 1 tsp mustard seeds
- ⚕ 1 cup split mung beans
- ⚕ 2 ½ -3 cups water

Heat ghee on medium heat and add spices. Cook until the spices' aroma comes up. Add split mung and stir to coat with ghee and spices. Add the water, stir, and bring to a boil. Reduce to simmer and cover with a lid for 30 minutes, or cook 15 minutes at pressure.

Tips: If you like dhal a little thinner, add another 1+ cup of water, and it will become soupy. In this thicker recipe it has the consistency of a dumpling. It will get thicker as the temperature cools.

Dhal with hijiki

serves 4 | preparation time: 30 minutes; with pressure cooker, 15-20 minutes | *Extractive*

- ⑥ 2 Tbsp ghee
- ⑥ ½ tsp mineral salt
- ⑥ 2+ tsp cumin seeds
- ⑥ ¼ tsp asafoetida
- ⑥ 1 cup split mung beans
- ⑥ 1 Tbsp hijiki
- ⑥ 3½ cups water

Heat ghee on medium heat and add mineral salt, cumin seed, and asafoetida. Cook until the spices' aroma comes up. Add split mung, hijiki, water and stir. Bring to a boil, reduce to simmer, and cover with a lid for 25 minutes, or cook 15 minutes at pressure.

Dhal with nori

serves 4 | preparation time: 25-30 minutes; with pressure cooker, 15-20 minutes | *Extractive*

- ⑥ 1-2 Tbsp ghee
- ⑥ 1 tsp mineral salt
- ⑥ 2 tsp cumin seeds
- ⑥ ¼ tsp asafoetida
- ⑥ 1 cup split mung beans
- ⑥ ¼ cup cut nori leaf
- ⑥ 3-4 cups water

Heat ghee on medium heat and add mineral salt, cumin seed, and asafoetida. Cook until the spices' aroma comes up. Add split mung, nori, water and stir. Bring to a boil, reduce to simmer, and cover with a lid for 20-25 minutes, or cook 15 minutes at pressure.

Garbanzo beans with coconut

serves 4 | preparation time: 45-50 minutes; with pressure cooker, 20 minutes | *Extractive*

- 1 cup garbanzo beans
- 1 Tbsp sesame oil
- ¼ tsp asafoetida
- ½ tsp mineral salt
- 1 stick kombu chopped small
- pinch powdered ginger
- 2 tsp powdered coriander
- ½ tsp ground cinnamon
- ½ tsp fresh ground black pepper or 10-12 black peppercorns
- water
- ½ cup fresh coconut milk

Combine all ingredients (except coconut milk) in pot. Add water to cover the beans by ⅓ inch and stir. Bring to a boil, reduce to simmer, and cover with a lid for 35-45 minutes, or cook 18 minutes at pressure. Add coconut milk after garbanzos are cooked.

Tips: Substitute 2-3 Tbsp of dried coconut reconstituted in water if fresh coconut milk is not available.

Garbanzo beans with sesame oil

serves 4 | preparation time: 40-45 minutes; with pressure cooker, 20 minutes | *Extractive*

- ⑥ 1 cup garbanzo beans
- ⑥ 1-2 Tbsp sesame oil
- ⑥ 1 Tbsp hijiki
- ⑥ 1 tsp fresh grated turmeric
- ⑥ ¾ tsp mineral salt
- ⑥ 2 tsp powdered cumin
- ⑥ 2 tsp powdered coriander
- ⑥ ¼ tsp powdered asafoetida
- ⑥ water

Combine all ingredients in pot. Add water to cover the beans by ⅓ inch and stir. Bring to a boil, reduce to simmer, and cover with a lid for 35-40 minutes, or cook 18 minutes at pressure.

Hummus

serves 4 | preparation time: 45-50 minutes; with pressure cooker, 20-25 minutes | *Extractive*

- ۞ 1 cup garbanzo beans
- ۞ 3 Tbsp sesame or olive oil
- ۞ 1 tsp mineral salt
- ۞ 1 tsp fresh grated ginger
- ۞ ¼ tsp powdered asafoetida
- ۞ water
- ۞ 2 Tbsp tahini
- ۞ 10 drops fresh lime juice
- ۞ ½ tsp fresh ground black pepper

Combine beans, 1 Tbsp oil, mineral salt, ginger, and asafoetida in pot. Add water to cover the beans by ⅓ inch and stir. Bring to a boil, reduce to simmer, and cover with a lid 30-40 minutes, or cook 18 minutes at pressure. Combine cooled beans in blender with 2 Tbsp oil, tahini, lime and black pepper. Add a little extra water if needed. Blend to desired consistency.

Adzukis may be combined with or substituted for the garbanzos as a variation.

Quinoa with dhal

serves 4 | preparation time: 30-35 minutes; with pressure cooker, 20 minutes | *Augmenting*

- ᛞ 2 Tbsp ghee
- ᛞ ½ tsp mineral salt
- ᛞ ½ tsp powdered turmeric
- ᛞ 2 tsp powdered cumin
- ᛞ 1½ cups quinoa
- ᛞ ¾ cup split mung beans
- ᛞ 4 ½ cups water

Heat ghee on medium heat and add spices. Cook until the spices' aroma comes up. Add rinsed quinoa, split mung, water and stir. Bring to a boil, reduce to simmer and cover with a lid for 25-30 minutes, or cook 18 minutes at pressure.

Rice and dhal with turmeric

serves 4 | preparation time: 30 minutes; with pressure cooker, 15-20 minutes | *Augmenting and Extractive*

- ⑥ 1¾ cups white basmati rice
- ⑥ ¾ cup split mung beans
- ⑥ 1-2 Tbsp ghee
- ⑥ 1 tsp mineral salt
- ⑥ ½ tsp powdered turmeric
- ⑥ 2 tsp cumin seeds
- ⑥ ½ tsp powdered asafoetida
- ⑥ 1-2 bay leaves
- ⑥ 5-6 cups water

Combine all ingredients in pot, stir, and bring to a boil. Reduce to simmer and cover with a lid for about 25 minutes, or cook about 15 minutes at pressure.

Tip: This recipe can be made in a soupy consistency by adding a bit more water.

Rice with dhal

serves 4 | preparation time: 40-45 minutes; with pressure cooker, 20 minutes | *Augmenting and Extractive*

- ۞ 2 Tbsp ghee
- ۞ ¾ tsp mineral salt
- ۞ 1 ½ tsp cumin seeds
- ۞ ¼ cup nori pieces
- ۞ 1 ¾ cups brown basmati rice
- ۞ ¾ cup split mung beans
- ۞ 5 cups water

Heat ghee on medium heat and add mineral salt and cumin seeds. Cook until the spices' aroma comes up. Add nori, rice, split mung, water and stir. Bring to a boil, reduce to simmer, and cover with a lid for 35-40 minutes, or cook 20 minutes at pressure.

Tip: This recipe is a great quick way to prepare the basis of a balanced meal. Choose an augmenting and extractive vegetable to complete the meal.

Sweet adzukis

serves 4 | preparation time: 40-45 minutes; with pressure cooker, 20 minutes | *Extractive*

- ⑥ 1 cup adzuki beans
- ⑥ 1 cup herbal chai tea (optional)
- ⑥ 2 Tbsp ghee
- ⑥ 1-2 tsp maple syrup
- ⑥ ¾ tsp mineral salt
- ⑥ ¼ tsp asafoetida
- ⑥ 1 tsp ground cinnamon
- ⑥ water

Combine all ingredients except maple syrup in pot. Add water to cover the beans by ⅓ inch and stir. Bring to a boil, reduce to simmer, and cover with a lid for 35-40 minutes, or cook 18 minutes at pressure. Add maple syrup after garbanzos are cooked.

Wild rice with dhal

serves 4 | preparation time: 45-50 minutes; with pressure cooker, 20 minutes | *Augmenting*

- ⚕ 1 ½ cups wild rice or blend
- ⚕ ⅔ cup split mung beans
- ⚕ 5 cups water
- ⚕ 2 tsp cumin seeds
- ⚕ 2 tsp fenugreek seeds
- ⚕ 2 Tbsp ghee
- ⚕ ¾ tsp mineral salt

Soak rice and split mung dhal 2-3 hours. Use soak water for cooking. Heat ghee on medium heat and add spices. Cook until the spices' aroma comes up. Stir in the soaking rice and dhal. Bring to a boil, reduce to simmer, and cover with a lid for 45 minutes, or cook 18 minutes at pressure.

ꞌVEGETABLES

In your daily meals, include a variety of fresh vegetables appropriate for your *dosha* and primarily *sattvic* (naturally balanced). Eat seasonal, locally grown vegetables. Vegetables can be cut, chopped or grated and combined with grains, spices, and herbs in endless combinations. Be creative within the principles.

Here are some tips in preparing and consuming vegetables:

    ⑥ Some popular vegetables are intentionally **not** included in these recipes. Refer to *Freedom in Your Relationship with Food* or halepule.com for lists of *sattvic* vegetables and caution about potatoes, tomatoes, eggplant, and bell peppers, for instance.

    ⑥ Consume vegetables with the juice they are cooked in. Sometime in the last 40 years, it became fashionable to cook vegetables in a dry manner - either with a small amount of oil or by steaming. In the first case, the vegetables become much drier. In the second case, the nutrients go into the water that isn't likely to be consumed. Today's living environments are extremely drying with air conditioning, heating, and chemical pollutants in the air. Eating dry food contributes significantly to many modern health problems.

⚇ While raw vegetables are popular these days, they aren't necessarily the best choice. Your *agni* must be strong enough to digest them or you will develop problems. The challenge of digesting raw food is accentuated in colder environments and particularly in the winter months. If you experience problems, choose cooked foods instead.

⚇ Turn off the heat 3-5 minutes before the vegetables are cooked and let the heat in the covered pan finish the cooking. It is easier to control the degree of cooking and is more energy efficient. Get to know your cooktop and pans, and the right timing will become obvious.

⚇ Pumpkins and squashes do not need to be peeled unless they are grown with chemicals or you are uncertain of their source. Sometimes with commercial squash the skin is tough and may need to be peeled.

⚇ Recipes in this book vary in terms of the amount of water recommended for cooking vegetables. It depends on the vegetable being cooked, but primarily on how much liquid you prefer. Some liquid is good, as it brings forth the qualities and taste of the spices and oil used, and provides additional moisture.

⚇ People often ask how long to cook the vegetables. Rather than adhering to a rigid formula, consider the strength of your *agni*, any imbalance in *vata*, and personal preference. Vegetables ought to be cooked enough so that the *prana* is accessible. This begins when the color starts to change with heating. With average or weak digestive fire and or *vata* imbalance, it is best to cook them a little more, until slightly soft. When experiencing any digestive disorder or recovering from illness, it is best to cook until the knife goes in easily. The length of time will vary according to the vegetables, size of pieces, pan, cooktop, and temperature in the environment.

⊛ There is no need to peel organically grown root vegetables. If you are not sure whether the plants were grown cleanly, peel.

⊛ This book suggests sweet potatoes, but yams may be used also. Yams do not offer as much nutritional value as sweet potatoes. Regular potatoes are in the nightshade family and not recommended. They tend to dull the mind and can contribute to joint difficulties in some constitutions.

⊛ Let your creativity flow! There are innumerable possibilities.

VEGETABLE RECIPES

Acorn squash

serves 4 | preparation time: 15-20 minutes |
Augmenting

- 3 cups chopped acorn squash
- 2 Tbsp ghee
- ¼ tsp ground cinnamon
- ¼ tsp mineral salt
- ½ tsp powdered ginger
- 1 ½ tsp powdered cumin
- water

Combine acorn squash in pot with ghee and spices.
Add water to ⅓ the level of squash. Bring to a boil with
lid on, reduce the heat, and simmer until squash is
soft.

Baked sweet potatoes

serves 4 | preparation time: 15-20 minutes |
Augmenting

- ⓦ 2-3 cups, ½-inch sliced sweet potatoes
- ⓦ 1-3 Tbsp liquid ghee
- ⓦ pinch ground cinnamon

Place sliced potatoes in glass baking dish. Add 3-4 drops of ghee to each slice. Sprinkle cinnamon over the potatoes. Bake at 300 until knife goes in easily.

Tips: Simmer in water instead of baking to maintain moisture. Coconut oil instead of ghee is a nice variation for summer.

Beets

serves 4 | preparation time: 15 minutes | *Augmenting*

- ⑥ 1 Tbsp ghee
- ⑥ 1 tsp fresh grated ginger
- ⑥ 2-3 cups chopped beets
- ⑥ water
- ⑥ ½ cup fresh chopped cilantro
- ⑥ ½ cup buttermilk

Heat ghee on medium heat and add ginger. Cook until the spices' aroma comes up. Add beets and stir to coat with ghee and ginger. Add water to ⅓ the level of beets, stir, and cover with a lid. Reduce the heat and simmer until beets are slightly soft or knife goes in easily. Stir in fresh cilantro and buttermilk just before serving.

Tip: Save the beet greens for another dish.

Beets, beet greens, with cottage cheese

serves 4 | preparation time: 20 minutes | *Augmenting and Extractive*

- ⑥ 2 Tbsp ghee
- ⑥ 1-2 tsp fresh grated ginger
- ⑥ 1 tsp fresh grated turmeric
- ⑥ ¾ tsp mineral salt
- ⑥ ½ tsp fresh ground black pepper
- ⑥ 3 cups chopped beets, beet stalk and beet greens
- ⑥ ½ cup fresh, whole cottage cheese or paneer
- ⑥ water

Heat ghee on medium heat and add spices. Cook until the spices' aroma comes up. Add beets and stems and stir to coat with ghee and spices. Simmer lightly for 2-3 minutes with lid on. Then add beet greens and water to ⅓ the level of vegetables, stir, and cover with a lid. Reduce the heat and simmer until greens are soft. Stir in cottage cheese after vegetables are cooked, just before serving.

Beets, beet greens with fresh chopped cilantro and parsley

serves 4 | preparation time: 10-15 minutes | *Augmenting and Extractive*

- ↻ 2 Tbsp ghee
- ↻ 1 tsp fresh grated ginger
- ↻ 1 tsp fresh grated turmeric
- ↻ ½ tsp mineral salt
- ↻ 1½ tsp coriander seeds
- ↻ ½ tsp cumin seeds
- ↻ 1 tsp fenugreek seeds
- ↻ ½ tsp mustard seeds
- ↻ 1 tsp fennel powder
- ↻ 3 cups chopped beets, stalks and greens
- ↻ ½ cup fresh chopped cilantro
- ↻ ½ cup fresh chopped parsley
- ↻ water

Heat ghee on medium heat and add ginger, turmeric, salt, spice seeds, and powder. Cook until the spices' aroma comes up. Add beets and simmer lightly 1-2 minutes with lid on. Then add greens and water to ½ level of beets, stir, and cover. Reduce the heat and simmer until beets and greens are slightly soft. Stir in cilantro and parsley at the end.

Tip: Mustard seeds are good for calming *vata* without aggravating *pitta*, and they assist in the digestion of protein.

Beet soup

serves 4 | preparation time: 20 minutes | *Augmenting*

- ⑥ 2 Tbsp coconut oil
- ⑥ 1-2 tsp fresh grated ginger
- ⑥ 1 tsp fresh grated turmeric
- ⑥ ¾ tsp mineral salt
- ⑥ 1-2 tsp cumin powder
- ⑥ 2 tsp coriander powder
- ⑥ ¼ tsp cinnamon powder
- ⑥ 3-4 cups chopped beets, stalks, and greens
- ⑥ water

Heat oil on medium heat and add spices. Cook until the spices' aroma comes up. Add beets and stir to coat with oil and spices. Simmer lightly for 3-5 minutes. Add stalks, beet greens and water to ½ the level of beets, stir, and cover with a lid. Reduce the heat and simmer until the beets are slightly soft. Remove from heat. Let cool and blend to desired soup consistency.

Tip: This goes nicely with a dollop of fresh paneer or fresh, whole cottage cheese.

Beets with carrot

serves 4 | preparation time: 10-15 minutes |
Augmenting

- ⑥ 1-2 Tbsp ghee
- ⑥ 1-2 tsp fresh grated ginger
- ⑥ ¾ tsp mineral salt
- ⑥ ½-1 tsp fresh ground black pepper
- ⑥ 1+ cup chopped beets
- ⑥ 1+ cup chopped carrots
- ⑥ ¼ cup fresh chopped cilantro
- ⑥ water

Heat ghee on medium heat and add ginger, salt, and black pepper. Cook until the spices' aroma comes up. Add cilantro, beets, and carrots, and stir to coat with ghee and spices. Add water to ¼ the level of vegetables, stir, and cover with a lid. Reduce the heat and simmer until vegetables are slightly soft.

Beets with cauliflower

serves 4 | preparation time: 15-20 minutes | *Augmenting and Extractive*

- ☺ 2 Tbsp ghee or oil
- ☺ 1 tsp cumin seeds
- ☺ 1 Tbsp coriander seeds
- ☺ 1 tsp fenugreek seeds or powder
- ☺ ½ tsp ginger powder
- ☺ ½ tsp turmeric powder
- ☺ ¾ tsp mineral salt
- ☺ 3 cups chopped beets
- ☺ 2-3 cups chopped cauliflower
- ☺ ½ cup fresh chopped cilantro or parsley
- ☺ water

Heat ghee or oil on medium heat and add cumin, coriander, fenugreek, ginger, turmeric, and salt. Cook until the spices' aroma comes up. Add beets and stir to coat with the ghee or oil and spices. Simmer for 2-3 minutes. Add cauliflower and water to ⅓ level of vegetables, stir, and cover with a lid. Reduce the heat and simmer until vegetables are slightly soft. Stir in cilantro or parsley near the end and let sit for 2-3 minutes.

Tip: Try substituting fennel seed or powder for the turmeric or adding a pinch of ajwain seeds for a different variation.

Bok choy, carrots with zucchini

serves 4 | preparation time: 15 minutes | *Extractive and Augmenting*

- ☉ 2 Tbsp ghee
- ☉ 1-2 tsp fresh grated ginger
- ☉ 1 tsp fresh grated turmeric
- ☉ ½ tsp fresh ground black pepper
- ☉ 1 tsp mustard seeds
- ☉ ½-¾ tsp mineral salt
- ☉ 2 cups chopped bok choy
- ☉ 1 cup chopped carrots
- ☉ 1 cup chopped zucchini
- ☉ 2 Tbsp cumin powder
- ☉ ½ cup fresh cilantro
- ☉ ¼-½ cup fresh parsley
- ☉ water

Heat ghee on medium heat and add ginger, turmeric, black pepper, mustard seeds, and salt. Cook until the spices' aroma comes up. Add bok choy, carrots, and zucchini, and stir to coat with ghee and spices. Add water to ¼ the level of vegetables, stir in cumin, cilantro, and parsley, and cover with a lid. Reduce the heat and simmer until vegetables are brighter in color or until slightly softer.

Broccoli and collards with shredded carrot

serves 4 | preparation time: 10-15 minutes | *Extractive*

- ⑥ 2 Tbsp ghee
- ⑥ ¾-1 tsp mineral salt
- ⑥ 1 tsp fresh ground turmeric
- ⑥ 1-2 tsp fresh chopped ginger
- ⑥ 2-3 cups chopped broccoli
- ⑥ 2-4 cups chopped collard greens
- ⑥ water
- ⑥ 1 small carrot grated
- ⑥ ¼ cup fresh cilantro

Heat ghee on medium heat and add spices. Cook until the spices' aroma comes up. Add broccoli and collards and stir to coat with ghee and spices. Add water to ½ the level of vegetables, stir, and cover with a lid. Reduce the heat and simmer until vegetables are lighter in color. Stir in the grated carrot and cilantro near the end and let sit for 2-3 minutes.

Broccoli, celery with Chinese cabbage

serves 4 | preparation time: 10-15 minutes | *Extractive*

- ෧ 1 Tbsp ghee
- ෧ ½ tsp mineral salt
- ෧ 2 tsp fresh grated ginger
- ෧ 1 tsp fresh grated turmeric
- ෧ ½ tsp fresh ground black pepper
- ෧ 2 tsp coriander seeds
- ෧ 2 cups chopped broccoli
- ෧ 1 cup chopped celery
- ෧ 1 cup chopped Chinese cabbage
- ෧ water

Heat ghee on medium heat and add spices. Cook until the spices' aroma comes up. Add broccoli, celery, and cabbage, and stir to coat with ghee and spices. Add water to ½ the level of the vegetables, stir, and cover with a lid. Reduce the heat and simmer until vegetables are brighter in color or until slightly soft.

Broccoli, cucumber with beet greens

serves 4 | preparation time: 15 minutes | *Extractive*

- ◌ 2 Tbsp ghee
- ◌ 1 ½ tsp fresh grated ginger
- ◌ 1 tsp fresh grated turmeric
- ◌ 1 tsp mineral salt
- ◌ Pinch of ajwain or celery seeds
- ◌ 3-4 cardamom pods
- ◌ 2 tsp cumin powder
- ◌ 1 tsp fresh ground black pepper
- ◌ 3 cups chopped broccoli
- ◌ 1½ cups peeled, chopped, and seeded cucumber
- ◌ 4 cups chopped beet greens and stems
- ◌ water

Heat ghee on medium heat and add spices. Cook until the spices' aroma comes up. Add vegetables and stir to coat with ghee and spices. Add water to ⅓ the level of vegetables, stir, and cover with a lid. Reduce the heat and simmer until vegetables are brighter in color.

Tip: Substitute cauliflower for broccoli. Be sure to cut vegetables a similar size, otherwise, add the larger pieces first, then the smaller pieces a few minutes later.

Broccoli, cucumber with zucchini

serves 4 | preparation time: 10-15 minutes | *Extractive*

- ⚬ 2+ Tbsp ghee
- ⚬ 1 tsp mineral salt
- ⚬ 2 tsp fresh grated ginger
- ⚬ 12 black peppercorns
- ⚬ 2 tsp coriander seeds
- ⚬ 2 tsp cumin seeds
- ⚬ 2-3 cups chopped broccoli
- ⚬ 1 cup peeled, seeded, and chopped cucumber
- ⚬ 1 cup chopped zucchini
- ⚬ water

Heat ghee on medium heat and add spices. Cook until the spices' aroma comes up. Add broccoli and stir to coat with ghee and spices. Simmer lightly for 1-2 minutes with lid on. Then add zucchini and cucumber. Add water to ½ the level of vegetables, stir, and cover with a lid. Reduce the heat and simmer until the vegetables are slightly soft.

Broccoli with Chinese cabbage

serves 4 | preparation time: 10-15 minutes | *Extractive*

- ⑥ 2+ Tbsp ghee
- ⑥ ¾ tsp mineral salt
- ⑥ pinch of powdered ginger
- ⑥ 1 tsp powdered cardamom
- ⑥ 1 Tbsp powdered coriander
- ⑥ ¼-½ cup lightly chopped pistachios (optional)
- ⑥ 1-2 cups chopped broccoli
- ⑥ 1-2 cups chopped Chinese cabbage
- ⑥ water

Heat ghee on medium heat and add spices. Cook until the spices' aroma comes up. Add broccoli and stir to coat with ghee and spices. Simmer lightly for 1-2 minutes with lid on. Then add cabbage, stir, and simmer for 1-2 minutes. Add water to ⅓ the level of vegetables, stir, and cover with a lid. Simmer until vegetable color is bright.

Tip: Substitute bok choy, tatsoi, or napa cabbage for the chinese cabbage

Broccoli with kale

serves 4 | preparation time: 20 minutes | *Extractive*

- ⚕ 2 Tbsp ghee
- ⚕ ½ tsp mineral salt
- ⚕ 1-2 tsp fresh grated ginger
- ⚕ 1-2 tsp fresh grated turmeric
- ⚕ 1 ½ tsp mustard seeds
- ⚕ 2 cups chopped broccoli
- ⚕ 2 cups chopped kale
- ⚕ water

Heat ghee on medium heat and add spices. Cook until the spices' aroma comes up. Add broccoli and kale and stir to coat with ghee and spices. Add water to ½ the level of vegetables, stir, and cover with a lid. Reduce the heat and simmer until vegetables are brighter in color or until slightly soft.

Cabbage with greens

serves 4 | preparation time: 15-20 minutes | *Extractive*

- ꙮ 1-2 Tbsp ghee, sesame, or sunflower oil
- ꙮ 2 cups chopped white cabbage
- ꙮ 1-2 tsp fresh grated ginger
- ꙮ 1-2 tsp fresh grated turmeric
- ꙮ ½ tsp mineral salt
- ꙮ ⅓ tsp asafoetida
- ꙮ 2-3 cups chopped dark greens
- ꙮ ½ tsp powdered cardamom
- ꙮ 1 ½ tsp powdered coriander
- ꙮ water

Heat ghee or oil on medium heat and add ginger, turmeric, salt, and asafoetida. Cook until the spices' aroma comes up. Add cabbage and stir to coat with ghee (or oil) and spices. Simmer lightly for 1-2 minutes with lid on. Then add greens and water to ⅓ the level of vegetables, stir, and cover with a lid for 2-3 minutes. Stir in cardamom and coriander and add more water if needed. Reduce the heat and simmer until greens are brighter in color or slightly soft.

Cabbage with collards

serves 4 | preparation time: 10-15 minutes | *Extractive*

- ⑥ 2+ Tbsp ghee
- ⑥ 1 ½ tsp cumin seeds
- ⑥ 2 tsp coriander seeds
- ⑥ 1 ½ tsp mustard seeds
- ⑥ 1-2 tsp fresh grated ginger
- ⑥ 1 tsp fresh turmeric
- ⑥ 1 tsp mineral salt
- ⑥ ½ tsp fresh ground black pepper
- ⑥ ½ tsp cardamom powder
- ⑥ ½-1 tsp tamarind paste
- ⑥ 2-3 cups chopped cabbage
- ⑥ 3 cups chopped collard greens
- ⑥ water

Heat ghee on medium heat and add cumin seeds, coriander seeds, mustard seeds, ginger, turmeric, salt, black pepper, and cardamom. Cook until the spices' aroma comes up and the mustard seeds just start to pop. Add cabbage and stir to coat with ghee and spices. Simmer lightly for 1 minute with lid on. Add a small amount of water and tamarind paste and stir. Then add collards, stir, and simmer for 1-2 minutes. Add water to ⅓ the level of vegetables, stir, and cover with a lid. Simmer for a few minutes.

Carrot ginger soup

serves 4 | preparation time: 20 minutes | *Augmenting*

- ◎ 3 cups chopped carrot
- ◎ 1 Tbsp ghee
- ◎ 2 tsp fresh grated ginger
- ◎ ¼ cup whole milk (optional)
- ◎ ½ cup fresh chopped cilantro
- ◎ ½ tsp fresh ground black pepper
- ◎ water

Cut carrots and add water to ¾ the level of them in the pot. Add ghee. Simmer until carrots are soft. Add the ginger. Cool a little. Place carrots and liquid in blender and add whole milk and cilantro. Blend until smooth or leave a few chunks of carrots. Stir in black pepper at the end.

Carrots, fennel with kale

serves 4 | preparation time: 15 minutes | *Augmenting*

- ⑥ 2 Tbsp ghee
- ⑥ 1 tsp fresh chopped ginger
- ⑥ 1 tsp fresh chopped turmeric
- ⑥ 2 tsp cumin powder
- ⑥ 2 tsp coriander powder
- ⑥ ½ tsp mineral salt
- ⑥ 2 cups chopped carrots
- ⑥ 1 cup fresh chopped fennel
- ⑥ 3 cups chopped kale
- ⑥ water

Heat ghee on medium heat and add ginger, turmeric, cumin, coriander, and salt. Cook until the spices' aroma comes up. Add carrots and fennel and stir to coat with ghee and spices. Add kale and water to ¼ the level of vegetables, stir, and cover with a lid. Reduce the heat and simmer until vegetables are brighter in color or until slightly softer.

Carrot with cucumber

serves 2-4 | preparation time: 5-10 minutes | *Augmenting*

- ⚙ 2 cups carrot and cucumber (peeled and seeded) cut into small sticks
- ⚙ 1-2 Tbsp sesame oil
- ⚙ 2-3 drops hot pepper sesame oil
- ⚙ ¼ tsp mineral salt
- ⚙ water

Sauté vegetables with oils, salt, and small amount of water until vegetables are brighter in color or slightly soft.

Tip: Leave off hot pepper sesame oil if you have excess pitta.

Chinese cabbage

serves 4 | preparation time: 10-15 minutes | *Extractive*

- Ⓖ 2 Tbsp coconut oil
- Ⓖ ½ tsp mineral salt
- Ⓖ ½ tsp black pepper
- Ⓖ 2 tsp coriander powder
- Ⓖ ¼ cup fresh chopped parsley
- Ⓖ 3-4 cups chopped Chinese cabbage
- Ⓖ water

Heat oil on medium heat and add spices. Cook until the spices' aroma comes up. Add cabbage and stir to coat with oil and spices. Simmer lightly 2-3 minutes with a lid on. Add water to ¼ the level of cabbage, stir, and cover with a lid. Reduce the heat and simmer until cabbage is slightly soft.

Chinese cabbage with pumpkin and pecans

serves 4 | preparation time: 10-15 minutes | *Extractive and Augmenting*

- ᴥ 2 Tbsp black sesame oil
- ᴥ 1 tsp fresh grated ginger
- ᴥ 1 tsp fresh grated turmeric
- ᴥ ½ tsp mineral salt
- ᴥ 1-2 tsp mustard seeds
- ᴥ 1 ½ tsp cumin seeds
- ᴥ 1 tsp coriander seeds
- ᴥ 3 cups chopped pumpkin squash
- ᴥ 2-3 cups chopped Chinese cabbage
- ᴥ ½ cup chopped pecans
- ᴥ water

Heat oil on medium heat and add spices. Cook until the spices' aroma comes up. Add pumpkin and pecans, and stir to coat with oil and spices. Cook 3-5 minutes, then add cabbage and water to ½ the level of vegetables, stir, and cover with a lid. Reduce the heat and simmer until vegetables are slightly soft.

Chinese cabbage with zucchini

serves 4 | preparation time: 10-15 minutes | *Extractive*

- ❺ 2 Tbsp black sesame oil
- ❺ 1 tsp fresh grated ginger
- ❺ 1 tsp fresh grated turmeric
- ❺ ½ tsp mineral salt
- ❺ 1-2 tsp mustard seeds
- ❺ 1 ½ tsp cumin seeds
- ❺ 3 cups chopped Chinese cabbage
- ❺ 2 cups chopped zucchini
- ❺ water

Heat oil on medium heat and add spices. Cook until the spices' aroma comes up. Add cabbage and zucchini and stir to coat with oil and spices. Add water to ½ the level of vegetables, stir, and cover with a lid. Reduce the heat and simmer until vegetables are slightly soft.

Collard greens

serves 4 | preparation time: 10-15 minutes | *Extractive*

- ⚬ 2 Tbsp ghee
- ⚬ 2 tsp fresh grated ginger
- ⚬ 1 tsp fresh grated turmeric
- ⚬ ½-¾ tsp mineral salt
- ⚬ 1 tsp coriander seeds
- ⚬ 1 tsp mustard seeds
- ⚬ ½ cup coarsely chopped cashews
- ⚬ 3-4 cups chopped collard greens
- ⚬ ¼ cup fresh chopped parsley
- ⚬ water

Heat ghee on medium heat and add ginger, turmeric, salt, mustard seeds, and cashews. Cook until the spices' aroma comes up. Add collard greens and stir to coat with ghee and spices. Add water to ½ the level of the collards, stir, and cover with a lid. Reduce the heat and simmer until greens are soft. Stir in parsley just before finishing cooking.

Corn off the cob with bok choy

serves 4 | preparation time: 15 minutes | *Augmenting and Extractive*

- ⚇ 2 Tbsp ghee
- ⚇ 1 Tbsp fresh grated ginger
- ⚇ 1 tsp fresh grated or powdered turmeric
- ⚇ 1-2 tsp cumin seeds
- ⚇ 1 tsp coriander seeds
- ⚇ 1 tsp fenugreek seeds
- ⚇ ¾ tsp mineral salt
- ⚇ 4-6 cups chopped bok choy
- ⚇ corn cut from 4 medium pieces of corn
- ⚇ pinch cinnamon powder

Heat ghee in pan and add ginger, turmeric, cumin, coriander, fenugreek, and salt. Cook until the spices' aroma comes up. Add bok choy and corn and stir to coat with ghee and spices. Add water to ⅓ the level of the vegetables, stir, and cover with a lid. Reduce the heat and simmer for 5-10 minutes. Add the pinch of cinnamon just before the end.

Dinosaur kale with carrot

serves 4 | preparation time: 10-15 minutes | *Extractive and Augmenting*

- ꙮ 2 Tbsp ghee
- ꙮ 1-2 tsp fresh grated ginger
- ꙮ 1 tsp fresh grated turmeric
- ꙮ ¾ tsp mineral salt
- ꙮ 3-4 cups chopped kale
- ꙮ 1 cup grated carrot
- ꙮ water

Heat ghee on medium heat and add spices. Cook until the spices' aroma comes up. Add kale and stir to coat with ghee and spices. Simmer lightly for 1 minute with lid on. Add water to ⅓ the level of kale, stir, and cover with a lid. Reduce the heat and simmer until kale is bright in color, then add grated carrot.

Green beans

serves 2-4 | preparation time: 5-10 minutes | *Extractive*

- ⑤ 2 cups cut green beans
- ⑤ water
- ⑤ ½ cup fresh chopped cilantro

Sauté green beans with small amount of water and cilantro until beans are brighter in color or slightly soft. Optionally add chopped pecans in the cooking process.

Green beans, cucumber with coconut

serves 4 | preparation time: 15 minutes | *Extractive*

- ⑥ 1-2 Tbsp ghee
- ⑥ 1 tsp powdered cumin
- ⑥ 1 tsp powdered coriander
- ⑥ ½ tsp turmeric
- ⑥ pinch of powdered ginger
- ⑥ ½ tsp mineral salt
- ⑥ 1½ cup cut green beans
- ⑥ ½ cup cucumber, peeled, seeded, and sliced in quarters
- ⑥ ½ cup shredded carrot
- ⑥ 1 tsp shredded coconut
- ⑥ water

Heat ghee on medium heat and add spices. Cook until the spices' aroma comes up. Add green beans and cucumber, and stir to coat with ghee and spices. Add water to ¼ the level of vegetables, stir, and cover with a lid. Reduce the heat and simmer until the beans are brighter in color. Stir in carrot and coconut near the end.

Green beans with chard

serves 4 | preparation time: 15 minutes | *Extractive*

- ⚉ 2+ Tbsp black sesame oil
- ⚉ 1-2 tsp fresh chopped ginger
- ⚉ 1 tsp mustard seeds
- ⚉ 2 Tbsp white sesame seeds
- ⚉ ½ tsp mineral salt
- ⚉ 2-3 cups chopped green beans
- ⚉ 2-3 cups chopped chard
- ⚉ water

Heat oil on medium heat and add spices. Cook until the spices' aroma comes up. Add green beans and stir to coat with oil and spices. Simmer lightly for 3-5 minutes. Add chard and water to ¼-½ the level of vegetables, stir, and cover with a lid. Reduce the heat and simmer until vegetables are brighter in color or until slightly softer.

Green beans with cucumber

serves 4 | preparation time: 10 minutes | *Extractive*

- ۶ 1-2 Tbsp ghee
- ۶ ½ tsp fresh grated ginger
- ۶ 1-2 tsp powdered cumin
- ۶ 1-2 tsp powdered coriander
- ۶ 3 cups bite size cuts of fresh green beans
  1 small cucumber, peeled, seeded, and chopped
- ۶ water

Heat ghee on medium heat and add spices. Cook until the spices' aroma comes up. Add vegetables and stir to coat with ghee and spices. Add water to ½ the level of vegetables and cover with a lid. Reduce the heat and simmer until vegetables are a brighter color or 3-8 minutes.

Tips: As a variation, add shredded carrot and/or cilantro for the last 2 minutes of cooking. To easily remove the cucumber seeds, quarter the cucumber long ways and then gently slice them off. Removal of the skin and seeds allows for easy digestion while retaining the benefits of the flesh.

Green beans with collards

serves 4 | preparation time: 10-15 minutes | *Extractive*

- ⑥ 2 Tbsp sesame oil
- ⑥ 1-2 tsp black sesame seeds
- ⑥ 1 Tbsp hijiki
- ⑥ ¾ tsp fresh grated turmeric
- ⑥ ½-1 tsp mineral salt
- ⑥ 1 tsp fresh grated ginger
- ⑥ ¾ cup chopped cashews
- ⑥ 2 cups chopped green beans
- ⑥ 2-3 cups chopped collard greens
- ⑥ 1 Tbsp tahini
- ⑥ 2 Tbsp fresh chopped parsley
- ⑥ 2-3 Tbsp fresh chopped cilantro
- ⑥ water

Heat one half of the sesame oil on medium heat and add spices and cashews. Cook until the spices' aroma comes up. Add vegetables and stir to coat with oil and spices. Add water to ½ the level of vegetables, stir, and cover with a lid. Reduce the heat and simmer until green beans are slightly soft. Stir in the fresh parsley and cilantro near the end of cooking. Mix the remaining sesame oil with tahini, and stir in at end.

Green beans with pecans

serves 4 | preparation time: 10 minutes | *Extractive*

- ☉ 1-2 Tbsp ghee
- ☉ ½ tsp mustard seeds
- ☉ ¾ tsp mineral salt
- ☉ ⅓ cup coarsely chopped pecans
- ☉ 2 cups chopped green beans
- ☉ water

Heat ghee on medium heat and add spices. Simmer until seeds begin to pop. Add pecans and green beans and stir to coat with ghee and spices. Add water to ⅓ the level of beans, stir, and cover with a lid. Reduce the heat and simmer until the beans are brighter in color or slightly soft.

Kale

serves 4 | preparation time: 10 minutes | *Extractive*

- ⚕ 1-2 Tbsp sesame or sunflower oil
- ⚕ 1 tsp fenugreek seeds
- ⚕ ½ tsp mineral salt
- ⚕ 4 cups chopped kale
- ⚕ water

Heat oil on medium heat and add spices. Cook until the spices' aroma comes up. Add kale and stir to coat with oil and spices. Add water to ⅓ the level of kale, stir, and cover with a lid. Reduce the heat and simmer until color deepens or leaves are slightly limp.

Kale, collard greens with celery

serves 4 | preparation time: 15 minutes | *Extractive*

- ⑥ 2 Tbsp ghee
- ⑥ ¾ tsp mineral salt
- ⑥ 1 tsp fresh grated ginger
- ⑥ 1 tsp fresh grated turmeric
- ⑥ 1 tsp mustard seeds
- ⑥ 2 cups chopped kale
- ⑥ 2 cups chopped collard greens
- ⑥ 1 cup chopped celery
- ⑥ water

Heat ghee on medium heat and add spices. Cook until the spices' aroma comes up. Add kale, collards, and celery, and stir to coat with ghee and spices. Add water to ⅓ the level of vegetables, stir, and cover with a lid. Reduce the heat and simmer until vegetables are slightly soft.

Tip: Substitute fresh fennel for celery.

Kale, sweet turnips with red cabbage

serves 4 | preparation time: 15-20 minutes | *Extractive*

- ⑥ 2 Tbsp ghee
- ⑥ 1-2 tsp fresh grated ginger
- ⑥ 1 tsp fresh grated turmeric
- ⑥ ¼ tsp fresh ground black pepper
- ⑥ 1-2 tsp brown mustard seeds
- ⑥ ½ tsp fenugreek seeds
- ⑥ ½ tsp mineral salt
- ⑥ 2 cups chopped kale
- ⑥ 1 cup chopped sweet turnips
- ⑥ 1 cup chopped red cabbage
- ⑥ ¼ cup fresh chopped cilantro
- ⑥ ¼ tsp ground cinnamon
- ⑥ water

Heat ghee on medium heat and add ginger, turmeric, black pepper, mustard seeds, fenugreek seeds, and salt. Cook until the spices' aroma comes up. Add kale, sweet turnips, and red cabbage, and stir to coat with ghee and spices. Add water to ¼ the level of vegetables, stir in cilantro and cinnamon, and cover with a lid. Reduce the heat and simmer until vegetables are brighter in color or until slightly softer.

Kale with fresh fennel

serves 4 | preparation time: 5-10 minutes | *Extractive*

- ⑥ 2 Tbsp coconut oil
- ⑥ 1-2 tsp fresh grated ginger
- ⑥ 1 tsp fresh grated turmeric
- ⑥ ¾ tsp mineral salt
- ⑥ ½ tsp fresh ground black pepper
- ⑥ ½-1 tsp mustard seeds
- ⑥ 2-4 cups chopped kale
- ⑥ ½-1 cup fresh finely chopped fennel
- ⑥ fresh coconut milk
- ⑥ 3-5 chopped curry leaves
- ⑥ 5-10 drops fresh squeezed lime
- ⑥ water

Heat coconut oil on medium heat and add ginger, turmeric, salt, black pepper, and mustard seeds. Cook until the spices' aroma comes up. Add fennel and kale and stir to coat with coconut oil and spices. Add water to ¼ the level of vegetables, stir, and cover with a lid. Reduce the heat and simmer until greens are deeper in color. Stir in coconut milk, curry leaves, and lime near the end.

Tip: Dried coconut with extra water may be substituted for the fresh.

Kale with ginger and turmeric

serves 4 | preparation time: 5-10 minutes | *Extractive*

- ⑥ 1-2 Tbsp ghee
- ⑥ 1-2 tsp fresh grated ginger
- ⑥ 1-2 tsp fresh grated turmeric
- ⑥ ½ tsp mineral salt
- ⑥ 1 tsp mustard seeds
- ⑥ 3-4 cups chopped kale
- ⑥ water

Heat ghee on medium heat and add spices. Cook until the spices' aroma comes up. Add kale and stir to coat with ghee and spices. Add ½ inch water, stir, and cover with a lid. Reduce the heat and simmer for a few minutes until the color of the kale is deeper green.

Kale with purple cabbage

serves 4 | preparation time: 10-15 minutes | *Extractive*

- ۞ 1-2 Tbsp ghee
- ۞ 1 tsp mineral salt
- ۞ 1 tsp fresh grated ginger
- ۞ 1 tsp fresh grated turmeric
- ۞ 1 tsp fenugreek seeds
- ۞ 12-15 black peppercorns
- ۞ 2 cups chopped kale
- ۞ 2-3 cups chopped purple cabbage
- ۞ ⅓-½ cup fresh chopped parsley
- ۞ ⅓ cup fresh chopped basil
- ۞ water

Heat ghee on medium heat and add salt, ginger, turmeric, fenugreek, and black peppercorns. Cook until aroma comes up. Add purple cabbage and kale and stir to coat with ghee and spices. Add water to ½ the level of vegetables, stir, and cover with a lid. Reduce the heat and simmer until deep color is present. Stir in fresh parsley and basil near the end of cooking.

Mixed vegetables

serves 4 | preparation time: 10-15 minutes | *Augmenting and Extractive*

- ⑥ 2 Tbsp ghee
- ⑥ 2 tsp fresh grated ginger
- ⑥ 1 tsp fresh grated turmeric
- ⑥ 1 tsp mustard seeds
- ⑥ 1 cup chopped broccoli
- ⑥ 1 cup chopped zucchini
- ⑥ 1 cup chopped carrot
- ⑥ 1 tsp cardamom powder
- ⑥ 2 tsp cumin powder
- ⑥ water

Heat ghee on medium heat and add ginger, turmeric, and mustard seeds. Cook until the spices' aroma comes up. Add broccoli, zucchini, and carrot, and stir to coat with ghee and spices. Add water to ⅓ the level of vegetables, stir in cardamom and cumin, and cover with a lid. Reduce the heat and simmer until vegetables are slightly soft.

Okra and kale

serves 4 | preparation time: 10-15 minutes | *Extractive*

- ⚅ 2+ Tbsp coconut oil
- ⚅ 1 tsp fresh ginger
- ⚅ 1 tsp fresh turmeric
- ⚅ ½ tsp dill seed
- ⚅ 1 tsp mustard seed
- ⚅ ¾ tsp mineral salt
- ⚅ 2 tsp cumin seed powder
- ⚅ 2 cups chopped okra
- ⚅ ¼ tsp cinnamon
- ⚅ 1-2 cups chopped kale or collard greens
- ⚅ water

Heat oil on medium and add ginger, turmeric, dill seed, mustard seed, mineral salt, and cumin powder. Cook until the spices' aroma comes up. Add okra and stir to coat with ghee and spices. Simmer lightly for 3-5 minutes. Add cinnamon, greens, and water to ⅓ the level of vegetables, stir, and cover with a lid. Reduce the heat and simmer until greens are brighter in color or until slightly softer.

Pumpkin carrot soup

serves 4 | preparation time: 20 minutes | *Augmenting*

- ⑥ 2 Tbsp ghee
- ⑥ 1 ½ tsp fresh grated ginger
- ⑥ ½ tsp fresh grated or powdered turmeric
- ⑥ 1 tsp mustard seed
- ⑥ 1-2 tsp coriander powder
- ⑥ 1 tsp cumin powder
- ⑥ ½ tsp cinnamon powder
- ⑥ ¾ tsp mineral salt
- ⑥ 4-5 cups chopped pumpkin or squash
- ⑥ 2-3 cups chopped carrots
- ⑥ handful of sprouts
- ⑥ water

Heat ghee on medium heat and add spices. Cook until the spices' aroma comes up. Add pumpkin and carrots and stir to coat with ghee and spices. Add water to ⅓ the level of the vegetables, stir, and cover with a lid. Reduce the heat and simmer until slightly soft. Remove from heat and cool enough to put into blender. When slightly cooled, blend one half or all of the vegetables in their own juice. Add additional liquid (water or herbal tea) to obtain the consistency you prefer. Add the sprouts when serving.

Pumpkin soup

serves 4 | preparation time: 15 minutes | *Augmenting*

- ⑥ 2 Tbsp ghee
- ⑥ 2 tsp fresh grated ginger
- ⑥ 1 tsp fresh grated turmeric
- ⑥ ½ tsp mineral salt
- ⑥ 1 tsp fresh ground black pepper
- ⑥ 1 tsp cumin seed
- ⑥ ½ tsp powdered cardamom
- ⑥ 3 cups chopped pumpkin
- ⑥ water

Heat ghee on medium heat and add spices. Cook until the spices' aroma comes up. Add pumpkin and stir to coat with ghee and spices. Add water to ½ the level of pumpkin, stir, and cover with a lid. Reduce the heat and simmer for 10-15 minutes or until pumpkin is soft. Blend all or part of pumpkin in a blender.

Pumpkin squash

serves 4 | preparation time: 15 minutes | *Augmenting*

- ⚕ 3-4 cups chopped pumpkin
- ⚕ 1 Tbsp ghee
- ⚕ 1 tsp fresh grated ginger
- ⚕ ½ tsp mineral salt
- ⚕ ¼-½ tsp ground cinnamon
- ⚕ ½ tsp coriander powder
- ⚕ water or herbal tea

Combine pumpkin, ghee, ginger, salt, cinnamon, and coriander in pot. Add water and/or herbal tea to ⅓ the level of pumpkin. Bring to a simmer with lid on, reduce the heat, and simmer for 5-10 minutes until pumpkin is soft.

Pumpkin squash with parsley

serves 4 | preparation time: 10-15 minutes | *Augmenting*

- ᘒ 1-2 Tbsp ghee
- ᘒ ½ tsp fresh grated or powder turmeric
- ᘒ 1 tsp fresh grated ginger
- ᘒ ½ tsp mineral salt
- ᘒ ½ tsp fresh ground black pepper
- ᘒ 3-4 cups cubed pumpkin
- ᘒ 1-2 Tbsp fresh chopped parsley
- ᘒ water

Heat ghee on medium heat and add spices. Cook until the spices' aroma comes up. Add cubed pumpkin and stir to coat with ghee and spices. Add water to ⅓ the level of pumpkin, stir, and cover with a lid. Reduce the heat and simmer gently for 10-15 minutes. Stir in fresh parsley near the end of cooking.

Purple cabbage with celery

serves 4 | preparation time: 15 minutes | *Extractive*

- ⑥ 2 Tbsp ghee
- ⑥ 1 tsp fresh grated ginger
- ⑥ 1 tsp fresh grated turmeric
- ⑥ 1 tsp fenugreek seeds
- ⑥ ½ tsp mineral salt
- ⑥ ½ tsp fresh ground black pepper
- ⑥ 2-3 cups chopped purple cabbage
- ⑥ 1 cup chopped celery
- ⑥ water

Heat ghee on medium heat and add spices. Cook until the spices' aroma comes up. Add cabbage and celery, and stir to coat with ghee and spices. Simmer lightly for 2-3 minutes with lid on. Add water to ⅓ the level of vegetables, stir, and cover with a lid. Reduce the heat and simmer until vegetables are brighter in color or until slightly soft.

Purple cabbage with collard greens

serves 4 | preparation time: 10-15 minutes | *Extractive*

- ⊚ 2-3 Tbsp black sesame oil
- ⊚ ½ tsp mineral salt
- ⊚ ½ tsp fresh ground black pepper
- ⊚ pinch powdered ginger
- ⊚ 1 ½ tsp mustard seeds
- ⊚ 2 cups chopped purple cabbage
- ⊚ 2 cups chopped collard greens
- ⊚ water
- ⊚ ¼ cup fresh chopped basil

Heat oil on medium heat and add salt, black pepper, ginger, and mustard seeds. Cook until the spices' aroma comes up. Add cabbage and collards, and stir to coat with oil and spices. Add water to ⅓ the level of vegetables, stir in basil, and cover with a lid. Reduce the heat and simmer until vegetables are lightly cooked.

Tip: If *pitta* is aggravated, use coconut oil, leave out black pepper, and use fresh ginger instead of powdered. Fresh ginger in moderation is balancing for all *doshas* and a great digestive aid. Powdered ginger is warming.

Red cabbage with sweet turnip

serves 4 | preparation time: 15 minutes | *Extractive*

- ⑥ 2 Tbsp ghee
- ⑥ 1-2 tsp fresh chopped ginger
- ⑥ 1 tsp fresh chopped turmeric
- ⑥ 2 tsp brown mustard seed
- ⑥ ½ tsp coriander seed
- ⑥ ¼ tsp fresh ground black pepper
- ⑥ ¾ tsp mineral salt
- ⑥ ¼ cup fresh chopped cilantro
- ⑥ 2 cups chopped red cabbage
- ⑥ 1 cup chopped sweet turnip
- ⑥ water

Heat ghee on medium heat and add ginger, turmeric, mustard seeds, coriander seed, black pepper and salt. Cook until the spices' aroma comes up. Add cilantro, red cabbage, and sweet turnip, and stir to coat with ghee and spices. Add water to ⅓ the level of vegetables, stir, and cover with a lid. Reduce the heat and simmer until vegetables are brighter in color or until slightly softer.

Tip: Reduce the amount of cabbage and include the turnip greens in this recipe, or just cook the turnips with their own greens in the same spices.

Simple beet greens

serves 4 | preparation time: 10-15 minutes | *Extractive*

- ◎ 2 Tbsp sesame oil
- ◎ 1 tsp cumin seeds
- ◎ ¾ tsp mineral salt
- ◎ 3-4 cups chopped beet greens
- ◎ water

Heat ghee on medium heat and add spices. Cook until the spices' aroma comes up. Add beet greens and stir to coat with oil and spices. Add water to ¼ the level of greens, stir, and cover with a lid. Reduce the heat and simmer until vegetables are brighter in color or until slightly softer.

Spiced carrots

serves 4 | preparation time: 15 minutes | *Augmenting*

- ⚕ 2 Tbsp ghee
- ⚕ 1 tsp fresh grated ginger
- ⚕ 1 tsp fresh grated turmeric
- ⚕ 1 tsp brown mustard seeds
- ⚕ 1 Tbsp black sesame seeds
- ⚕ 2 tsp hijiki
- ⚕ ½ tsp mineral salt
- ⚕ 2-3 cups chopped carrots
- ⚕ ½ cup chopped cilantro
- ⚕ ¼ tsp cumin powder
- ⚕ water

Heat ghee on medium, add ginger, turmeric, mustard seeds, sesame seeds, hijiki, and salt. Cook until the spices' aroma comes up. Add carrots and stir to coat with ghee and spices. Add water to ¼ the level of carrots, stir in cilantro and cumin, and cover with a lid. Reduce the heat and simmer until vegetables are brighter in color or until slightly softer.

Sweet potato in a crust

serves 4 | preparation time: 1 hour | *Augmenting*

Sweet potatoes

- ⚇ 2-3 cups chopped sweet potatoes
- ⚇ 2 Tbsp ghee
- ⚇ water

Combine sweet potatoes and ghee in pot. Add water to ½ the level of sweet potatoes. Bring to a boil with lid on, reduce the heat, and simmer until sweet potatoes are soft. Either blend all of the potatoes with the liquid, or blend a portion and mix with the remaining pieces.

Crust

- ⑥ 2 ½ cups freshly ground rice flour
- ⑥ ½ cup flax meal (ground flax seeds)
- ⑥ pinch mineral salt
- ⑥ 1½ Tbsp ghee
- ⑥ ½ cup coarsely chopped pistachios
- ⑥ water

Mix flour, flax, and salt. Stir in ghee, and then add water to create moist dough. Let sit covered for 5 minutes. Press into a baking dish. Bake crust five minutes at 300 or until warm and slightly crisp on top, then add potatoes. Sprinkle pistachios on top.

Tip: Substitute peeled, chopped almonds or macadamia nuts for pistachios.

Sweet potatoes mashed with cinnamon

serves 4 | preparation time: 15 minutes | *Augmenting*

- ⑥ 3-4 cups cubed sweet potatoes
- ⑥ 1 tsp ghee
- ⑥ ½-1 tsp ground cinnamon
- ⑥ water

Bring potatoes to a simmer in pot with ghee, cinnamon, and water (⅓ the level of potatoes). Cover with a lid and cook gently until potatoes are soft. Remove from heat and mash. Add a little more water as needed.

Tip: Using an herbal tea such as rooibos chai in place of the water or part of the water adds interesting flavor to this dish.

Add a pinch of nutmeg or use a cinnamon stick instead of ground cinnamon.

The potato may also be left in cubes, unmashed and eaten with just a touch of ghee.

Sweet potatoes with cashews

serves 4 | preparation time: 10-15 minutes | *Augmenting*

- 1 Tbsp ghee
- 1 tsp black sesame seeds
- 1 tsp cumin powder
- pinch mineral salt
- ½ cup chopped cashews
- 3-4 cups chopped sweet potatoes
- ½ cup fresh chopped parsley
- ½ cup fresh chopped cilantro
- water

Heat ghee on medium heat and add spices and cashews. Cook until the spices' aroma comes up. Add the sweet potatoes, parsley, and cilantro, and stir to coat with ghee and spices. Add water to ¼-⅓ the level of sweet potatoes, stir, and cover with a lid. Reduce the heat and simmer until sweet potatoes are soft. The potatoes may be eaten in chunks or mashed.

Sweet potato with Chinese cabbage

serves 4 | preparation time: 15 minutes | *Augmenting and Extractive*

- ⑥ 2 Tbsp black sesame oil
- ⑥ 1 tsp fresh grated ginger
- ⑥ 1 tsp fresh grated turmeric
- ⑥ 1 tsp black or white sesame seeds
- ⑥ ½ tsp mineral salt
- ⑥ ¼ tsp fresh ground black pepper
- ⑥ 2-3 cups chopped sweet potatoes
- ⑥ 2 cups chopped Chinese cabbage
- ⑥ 1 Tbsp tahini
- ⑥ water

Heat oil on medium heat and add spices. Cook until the spices' aroma comes up. Add sweet potatoes and stir to coat with oil and spices. Add just enough water to cover the bottom of the pot, and simmer lightly 2-5 minutes with lid on. Then add cabbage and water to ⅓ the level of vegetables, stir, and cover with a lid. Reduce the heat and simmer until vegetables are soft. Stir in tahini at end.

Sweet potatoes with fresh coconut meat

serves 4 | preparation time: 10-15 minutes | *Augmenting*

- ⑤ 1 Tbsp ghee
- ⑤ 1 tsp fresh grated ginger
- ⑤ pinch mineral salt
- ⑤ 1 tsp coriander powder
- ⑤ ½ tsp fresh ground black pepper
- ⑤ 4 cups chopped sweet potatoes
- ⑤ 1 cup fresh coconut milk (blend meat with coconut water leaving chunky or to smooth consistency)
- ⑤ water

Heat ghee on medium heat and add spices. Cook until the spices' aroma comes up. Add chopped sweet potatoes and stir to coat with ghee and spices. Simmer for 3-5 minutes. Add coconut milk and water to ¼ the level of sweet potatoes, stir, and cover with a lid. Reduce the heat and simmer until potatoes are soft.

Tip: Additional coconut milk may be used instead of water. The potatoes may be eaten in chunks or mashed. Substitute 2-4 Tbsp unsweetened coconut flakes if fresh is not available; just add extra water to about ⅓ the level of sweet potatoes.

Sweet potatoes with herbal chai tea

serves 4 | preparation time: 10-15 minutes | *Augmenting*

- ⑥ 2-3 cups chopped sweet potatoes
- ⑥ 1 Tbsp ghee
- ⑥ 1 cup herbal chai tea
- ⑥ water

Combine potatoes and ghee in pot. Add water and herbal tea to ½ the level of sweet potatoes. Bring to a boil with lid on, reduce the heat, and simmer until potatoes are soft.

Sweet potatoes with rose petals

serves 4 | preparation time: 15 minutes | *Augmenting*

- ⚬ 1 Tbsp ghee
- ⚬ ⅛ tsp mineral salt
- ⚬ ½ tsp ground cinnamon
- ⚬ tiny pinch of clove
- ⚬ 3-4 cups chopped sweet potatoes
- ⚬ 10-15 rose petals
- ⚬ water

Heat ghee on medium heat and add spices. Cook until the spices' aroma comes up. Add sweet potatoes and stir to coat with ghee and spices. Add water to ½ the level of sweet potatoes, stir, and cover with a lid. Reduce the heat and simmer until potatoes are soft. Stir in the rose petals near the very end.

Tip: Rose petals may be fresh or dried. Be sure that they are organically grown, without pesticides, herbicides, or chemical fertilizers.

Zucchini

serves 4 | preparation time: 5-10 minutes | *Augmenting*

- ⚕ 2 Tbsp ghee
- ⚕ 1 tsp fresh grated ginger
- ⚕ 1 tsp fresh grated turmeric
- ⚕ ½ tsp mineral salt
- ⚕ 1-2 tsp coriander seeds
- ⚕ ½ tsp fresh ground black pepper
- ⚕ ½ tsp powdered cardamom
- ⚕ 3-4 cups chopped zucchini
- ⚕ water

Heat ghee on medium heat and add spices. Cook until the spices' aroma comes up. Add zucchini and stir to coat with ghee and spices. Add water to ⅓-½ the level of the zucchini, stir, and cover with a lid. Reduce the heat and simmer until a slight color change occurs, then turn off the heat and allow cooking to continue for 2-3 minutes.

Zucchini with purple cabbage

serves 4 | preparation time: 15 minutes | *Augmenting and Extractive*

- ⑥ ½ tsp black cumin oil
- ⑥ 1 Tbsp black sesame oil
- ⑥ 1 tsp fresh grated ginger
- ⑥ 1 tsp fresh grated turmeric
- ⑥ 1 Tbsp black sesame seeds
- ⑥ 1 tsp fenugreek seeds
- ⑥ ½ tsp mineral salt
- ⑥ 5-10 black peppercorns
- ⑥ 2 cups chopped zucchini
- ⑥ 1-2 cups chopped purple cabbage
- ⑥ 1 Tbsp tahini
- ⑥ 5 drops fresh lime juice
- ⑥ water

Heat oils on medium heat and add ginger, turmeric, spice seeds, salt, and peppercorns. Cook until the spices' aroma comes up. Add zucchini and cabbage and stir to coat with oil and spices. Simmer lightly 1-2 minutes with a lid on. Add water to ⅓ the level of vegetables, stir, and cover with a lid. Reduce the heat and simmer until vegetables change color or until slightly soft. Stir in tahini and lime after cooking.

LIGHT MEALS, SIDES, AND DRINKS

Light meals are beneficial with a long stretch between meals. For example, eat lunch at eleven a.m., then a snack at two or three p.m., and a light dinner at five-thirty p.m. They are also useful when you are feeling compromised and a full meal feels like too much to digest.

Light meals and drinks require a complete digestive cycle, just as a full meal does. The body must have time to completely digest the previous meal before consuming more food or drink or there will be negative consequences in your health.

LIGHT MEALS

Coconut carob muffins

serves 4-8 | preparation time: 25 minutes mostly unattended | *Slightly augmenting*

- ☙ 3 cups wheat flour
- ☙ ¼ cup mesquite flour
- ☙ ½ cup coconut flour

- ⚬ 3 Tbsp carob powder
- ⚬ 1 tsp mineral salt
- ⚬ 1 tsp sweet cinnamon powder
- ⚬ 1 tsp cardamom powder
- ⚬ ¼ cup coconut oil
- ⚬ ¼ cup maple syrup
- ⚬ 1-2 handfuls of raisins (reconstitute in advance)
- ⚬ apple juice, apple sauce, or water

Combine all dry ingredients. Add oil, maple syrup, and raisins. Add apple juice, applesauce, and/or water until it is slightly sticky dough. Gently pinch a ball of dough into desired size of muffins. Allow them to be irregular in shape and avoid handling too much. Bake at 350 for 15-20 minutes.

Tips: Baking time will depend on the oven, room temperature, and size of muffins. Be mindful not to overcook, as this will dry the muffins out. For additional sweetness, dribble on honey (for *vata* or *kapha*) or maple syrup (for *pitta*).

Cooked apples

serves 4 | preparation time: 10 minutes | *Augmenting*

- 2 small to medium apples
- 1-2 Tbsp ghee
- 1 tsp cinnamon powder
- ¾ tsp cardamom powder
- pinch of mineral salt

Slice apples into cubes or strips, and combine in pot with small amount of ghee and spices, as you like. Experiment with various combinations of cinnamon powder, cardamom powder, fresh mint, or fresh grated ginger. Add water to ⅓ the level of the apples and simmer until a knife goes in easily. You may cook the spices first or simmer all ingredients together.

Tips: For applesauce, cook until apples may be easily mashed or put into a blender.

Cooling fruit pie

serves 4 | preparation time: 1 hour | *Augmenting*

Filling

- ⑥ 3 cups fresh chopped stone fruit or berries
- ⑥ 1-2 Tbsp coconut oil
- ⑥ 1 Tbsp maple syrup (optional)
- ⑥ 1 tsp sweet cinnamon powder
- ⑥ ½ tsp cardamom powder
- ⑥ water

Combine all ingredients in a blender with a small amount of water or herbal chai tea. Use one or two types of fruit at most. If the fruit is sweet then leave out the maple syrup.

Crust

- ⑥ 2 cups flour
- ⑥ ¼ cup ground flax
- ⑥ 1 tsp mineral salt
- ⑥ 2+ Tbsp ghee
- ⑥ water

Mix flour, flax, and mineral salt. Stir in ghee and then water to form soft dough. Press into a glass baking dish and bake at 300 for 5-10 minutes. Add a little more ghee if the crust seems dry. Add fruit filling to cooked crust and let sit for 10 minutes to thicken. Enjoy!

Dates soaked in ghee

serves 4 | preparation: 5 minutes | *Augmenting*

- ൠ 8 dates
- ൠ Ghee
- ൠ ¼-½ tsp cardamom powder (optional)
- ൠ ¼-½ tsp cinnamon powder (optional)

Slice the dates in half and remove the pits. Pour enough warm ghee to cover the dates. Add spice if you'd like, such as ¼-½ tsp cardamom and/or ¼-½ tsp cinnamon. Soak for 1 day to 2 weeks. Will keep indefinitely without contamination of the ghee.

Tips: You can also fill a jar with dates, pour ghee over them, and store in the pantry for future use. Medicinal herbs may also be added. Dates are good for increasing vitality and strengthening immunity. Remember, moderation if you tend toward sugar cravings.

LIGHT MEALS, SIDES, AND DRINKS

Muffins

serves 4-8 | preparation time: 25 minutes mostly unattended | *Augmenting*

- ⑥ 1 ½ cups of whole wheat flour
- ⑥ 1 ½ cup of rice flour
- ⑥ ¾ cups coconut flour
- ⑥ 2 Tbsp flax meal
- ⑥ 1 tsp cardamom powder
- ⑥ 1 ½ tsp cinnamon powder
- ⑥ ¼ tsp nutmeg powder
- ⑥ ¼ tsp ginger powder
- ⑥ 1 tsp salt
- ⑥ 1 cup raisins
- ⑥ 2 small apples chopped
- ⑥ 2-3 Tbsp ghee
- ⑥ apple juice, water or herbal tea

Mix flours, spices, mineral salt, raisins, apples, and ghee thoroughly. Add water or apple juice until the mixture comes to slightly sticky dough. Bake at 350 for 15-18 minutes. Cook time will vary depending on size of the balls, the pan, and the oven. The best test is to insert a toothpick until it comes out clean.

Tips: Raisins will taste better and be easier to digest if reconstituted in a small amount of water for 1-2 hours before cooking. Use the liquid from the raisins in the muffins. Substitute chopped nuts and extra ghee for the raisins and apples.

Parsnip snack

serves 4 | preparation time: 10 minutes | *Augmenting*

- ⑥ 1-2 Tbsp ghee
- ⑥ ½ tsp mineral salt
- ⑥ 1 tsp mustard seeds
- ⑥ ¼-½ cup shredded coconut
- ⑥ 2 cups sliced parsnip
- ⑥ water

Heat ghee and stir in mineral salt, mustard seeds, and coconut. Simmer until the spices' aroma comes up. Stir in parsnip and simmer gently for 3-5 minutes. Add a small amount of water as needed. Eat warm or room temperature. This recipe works well with sweet potatoes too.

Quick roll up

serves 1 | <5 minutes | *Augmenting and Extractive*

- Ⓖ 1 small avocado
- Ⓖ 2-4 Tbsp fresh, whole cottage cheese or paneer
- Ⓖ pinch fresh ground black pepper
- Ⓖ pinch cumin powder
- Ⓖ 1 brown rice tortilla or chapati
- Ⓖ 1 handful clover sprouts

Mash avocado and cottage cheese together with black pepper and cumin powder. Roll in warmed tortilla with sprouts. Adding a few soaked chopped almonds is another option.

Quinoa balls

serves 2-4 | preparation time: 10 minutes | *Augmenting*

- ⑥ 1 cup cooked split mung beans , room temperature
- ⑥ 1 cup cooked quinoa, room temperature
- ⑥ ghee, sesame oil, or coconut oil

Form split mung into balls; coat with cooked quinoa. Warm in a pan oiled with ghee, sesame, or coconut oil or in the oven.

Tips: Eat with nori wrap and avocado. Or, make a sauce with tahini, water, basil, and a splash of lime to accompany.

Spiced plantain

serves 4 | preparation time: 10-15 minutes | *Augmenting*

- ◍ 2-3 Tbsp ghee
- ◍ ½ tsp mineral salt
- ◍ ½ tsp cumin seeds
- ◍ ½ tsp fennel seeds
- ◍ ¼ tsp fresh ground black pepper
- ◍ pinch cinnamon powder
- ◍ 2 cups chopped plantain
- ◍ water (as needed)

Heat ghee and stir in mineral salt, cumin, fennel, black pepper, and cinnamon. Simmer until the spices' aroma comes up. Stir in plantain and simmer until knife goes in easily. Add a small amount of water as needed. Eat warm or room temperature.

Tip: Plantain is also nice combined with augmenting vegetables, such as carrot or zucchini.

Sweet potato snack

serves 4 | preparation time: 10 minutes | *Augmenting*

- ☉ 1-2 Tbsp coconut oil or ghee
- ☉ ¼ tsp mineral salt
- ☉ ½ tsp sweet cinnamon powder
- ☉ pinch clove powder
- ☉ ½ tsp fresh chopped ginger
- ☉ 2 cups chopped sweet potato

Heat oil or ghee and simmer spices until spices' aroma comes up. Add water to ¼ level of the sweet potatoes and simmer gently until color is brighter or knife goes in easily.

SIDES

Chapati (basic)

serves 4 | preparation time: 15 minutes | *Augmenting*

- ⑥ 3 cups flour
- ⑥ ¾ tsp mineral salt
- ⑥ 1-2 tsp ghee
- ⑥ water

Stir flour, mineral salt, and ghee together. Add water until mixture becomes a consistent, slightly sticky dough. Break off a golf-ball-sized piece and roll into a ball using the palms of the hands. Set the balls aside in order, so that you can roll out the oldest one first. It is helpful for the balls to sit a couple of minutes, but not too long as they will dry out.

Bring a medium size pan to low-medium heat with a small amount of ghee while you are rolling the chapati.

Place flour on a board and roll each ball into a very thin pancake size shape using a rolling pin. Roll them as thin as possible. Don't worry if yours are not round. It takes practice and oblong chapatis taste just as great. Rolling vertically then horizontally helps with the shape. Add extra flour if needed to keep the dough from sticking to the board or rolling pin. Dust the finished chapatis with flour so that they can lie atop another without sticking together.

Place the first chapati in the pan to cook while you are rolling the others. It helps to place the board right next to the cooktop. Employ someone to roll while you cook for quicker preparation.

Simmer the chapati 1-3 minutes on each side. The time will depend on your pan and cooktop. Add a little more ghee after each chapati. If the pan is large enough, cook two at a time.

Place finished chapatis in a covered dish. Additional ghee may be added if you like.

This entire process can be done with your hands, without utensils. Try it! There are also small rolling pins specially designed for making chapatis.

Tips: Choose from a variety of flours, such as whole wheat, whole wheat and rice, barley, or barley and rice. You can also add a small amount of coconut flour to any of the previous flours. Use wheat or barley as the primary flour to help hold the chapati together. About ⅓ rice or coconut flour will give an interesting flavor and texture variation. Grind your own flour from whole grains for maximum life force and taste. Hand or electric grain mills are a great, easy-to-use kitchen tool. The freshness of the flour is reflected in the taste of the chapati.

Chapati Variations

Cottage cheese chapati

Augmenting

Roll out basic chapati and spread with a thin layer of fresh, whole cottage cheese, paneer, or goat cheese and sprinkle of fresh ground black pepper. Fold in half and gently roll a second time.

Macadamia nut chapati

Augmenting and Extractive

¼-½ cup chopped macadamia nuts

Add nuts to flour before making the dough or roll the chapati, add the nuts, fold it over and roll again.

Spiced chapati

Augmenting

- ◉ 1 tsp cumin seeds
- ◉ ½ tsp fennel seeds

Add seeds to flour before making the dough.

Veggie chapati

Augmenting

Roll out basic chapati and sprinkle with grated veggies such as carrot, beet, or zucchini. Fold in half and gently roll a second time.

Dosas

serves 4 | preparation time: 10 minutes | *Augmenting and Extractive*

- ৬ 1 ½ cup white or brown basmati rice
- ৬ 2/3 cup split mung beans or 1/3 cup split mung and 1/3 cup urad dhal
- ৬ 1–1½ cups of water
- ৬ 1 tsp mineral salt
- ৬ Ghee (enough to coat pan)

Soak rice and dhal separately in bowls of water overnight or for at least 6 hours. Rinse thoroughly. Put in blender with mineral salt. Blend, adding enough water to make a batter. Coat pan with ghee and cook the batter like small, thin pancakes on medium heat.

Tips: Add a hint of cinnamon powder for augmenting flavor. Serve with cottage cheese, vegetables, or tahini and honey. These also make a complete breakfast.

Guacamole

serves 4 | preparation time: 5 minutes | *Augmenting*

- ☉ 2 small avocados
- ☉ 10-12 drops fresh squeezed lime
- ☉ ½ tsp fresh ground black pepper
- ☉ 5-10 chili pepper flakes

Mash avocado. Add lime, pepper, and chili pepper flakes. Mix well.

Tip: You can substitute ⅓tsp cayenne pepper for chili flakes or leave them out altogether.

Guacamole with dill

serves 4 | preparation time: 5 minutes | *Augmenting*

- ☉ 2 medium avocado
- ☉ 8 flakes chili pepper (seeds)
- ☉ ¼ tsp dill seeds
- ☉ 4-6 drops fresh squeezed lime juice
- ☉ ¼ cup fresh cilantro

Mash avocado. Add all ingredients, mixing well. May be served with fresh clover sprouts.

Pesto

serves 2-4 | preparation time: 5 minutes | *Augmenting and Extractive*

- ⑥ 1-2 bunches basil
- ⑥ ½ cup olive oil
- ⑥ ½+ cup water
- ⑥ ¼ cup macadamia nuts
- ⑥ 1-2 Tbsp tahini
- ⑥ ½ tsp mineral salt

Combine all ingredients into blender and blend. More water or oil may be desired for consistency.

Tips: Mix this pesto with a grain, such as pearl barley or brown rice left over from lunch. For *vata* aggravation, use basil, olive oil, water, and mineral salt. For *pitta* aggravation, substitute coconut oil and use basil, 1-2 bunches fresh cilantro, and mineral salt. For *kapha* aggravation, substitute sunflower oil and use basil, 1-2 bunches fresh parsley, mineral salt, and ½-1 tsp fresh ground black pepper.

Paneer (fresh cheese)

serves 8 | preparation time: 45 minutes | *Augmenting*

- ↺ ½ gallon whole milk
- ↺ 10-15% of milk volume of fresh squeezed lemon juice

Place milk in pot and bring slowly to a boil. Add lemon juice slowly allowing milk to become solid. Add more lemon only as needed to continue solidifying the milk. Let it sit a while (15 minutes +) to be sure the curdling is complete. Strain the curdled milk through unbleached cheesecloth, squeezing at the end to remove remaining liquid. Place cheese in glass or ceramic container. If you'd prefer square-cut pieces, press to the shape of the container. Otherwise leave it irregular. Eat with cooked veggies.

Spicy tahini sauce

serves 4 | preparation time: 5 minutes | *Extractive*

- ✆ 2 Tbsp raw tahini
- ✆ 1 Tbsp sesame oil
- ✆ 4 drops of hot pepper sesame oil
- ✆ 3-5 drops fresh lime juice

Blend ingredients by hand.

Tahini dressing

serves 4-8 | preparation time: 5 minutes | *Augmenting and Extractive*

- ✆ herbal tea
- ✆ ½ cup tahini
- ✆ 1-2 Tbsp sesame oil
- ✆ 5-10 drops lime juice

Combine all ingredients in a bowl and blend well.

Tip: Honeybush is a nice herbal tea to use in this tahini.

Wasabi (Japanese horseradish)

Add small amounts of wasabi to sushi. It can be purchased fresh, in powder form, or as a paste. Reconstitute the powder with a pinch of water. Small amounts of wasabi are okay for *vata* and *kapha*. Best avoided by those with *pitta* aggravation or tendency toward *pitta* imbalance. Fresh wasabi in small amounts is okay for balanced pitta.

Tip: You can also season with ume plum paste, which can be purchased at most health food stores. It is a fermented product and appropriate in small quantities.

❧

DRINKS

Fruit smoothie

serves 4 | preparation time: 5 minutes | *Augmenting*

- ⚕ 2-4 cups of 1, 2, or 3 fresh fruits
- ⚕ ½ tsp fresh chopped ginger
- ⚕ ¼ tsp cinnamon powder

Combine 2 or 3 maximum room-temperature fresh fruits with herbal tea or water and blend. The water or herbal tea can be warm. Add small amounts of ginger and/or cinnamon to aid digestion.

Tips: Adding too many fruits or other ingredients complicate digestion. Best to keep it simple and enjoy each distinct flavor. Add chopped dates or soaked raisins for increased vitality and to enhance the sweet taste. Use warm or room temperature herbal tea for a nice breakfast or snack.

Lassi

serves 4 | preparation time: 5 minutes | *Augmenting*

- ☉ 2 cups plain yogurt (preferably fresh made)
- ☉ 2 cups water
- ☉ ½ tsp cumin powder
- ☉ ½ tsp coriander powder
- ☉ ¼ tsp fennel powder
- ☉ ⅓ tsp fresh ground black pepper

Combine in a blender and blend or simply stir.

Tip: Use ½ tsp turmeric powder, ¼ tsp fresh ground black pepper, ¼ tsp mineral salt, and 4-8 fresh mint leaves or rose petals and blend.

Nighty-night nightcap

serves 1 | preparation time: 5 minutes | *Augmenting*

- ½-1 cup whole milk
- ½ tsp ghee
- ½-1 tsp cardamom powder
- ½-1 tsp cinnamon powder
- 1-2 tsp honey
- pinch fresh ground nutmeg

Warm the milk and ghee with cardamom and cinnamon. Place honey in bottom of drinking cup. Add warm mixture to it. Do not use the same amount of honey and ghee by volume as it causes disturbance in digestion. Add fresh ground nutmeg (has a sedative quality) to support peaceful sleep.

Tips: Cardamom is useful in reducing milk's mucous-forming tendency. Sip this nightcap just before bed in order to fall easily and deeply asleep. Modify and use cumin, coriander, and cardamom for a more cooling effect. If *pitta* is aggravated, use maple syrup or sucanat instead of honey for sweetening. Add a pinch of fresh vanilla bean for additional grounding and flavor. Milk may be boiled first for easier digestion. Use raw milk whenever possible.

Teas

Soak loose tea in water overnight, ideally. Bring to boil and turn off heat. Only herbal teas are recommended in this book, as stimulants and caffeinated products over stimulate the nervous system and do not promote well-being.

These suggested combinations aid digestion and are very pleasant to the palate. Explore other combinations, using the best local ingredients, with consideration of the qualities, such as warming and cooling. Remember, moderation is the key to bringing balance and well-being. Following cravings is moving toward imbalance.

- Vanilla rooibos tea, fresh sliced ginger
- Rooibos, hibiscus
- Honeybush, fresh sliced ginger
- Herbal chai tea mix, with or without fresh ginger slices
- Fresh sliced ginger, licorice powder
- Fresh sliced ginger, fresh mint leaves, cardamom pods or powder
- Coriander powder, licorice
- Coriander, cardamom, turmeric powders
- Coriander, cardamom, fresh sliced ginger

Tips: Add honey (warming) or maple syrup (cooling) to the steeping tea. Raisins boiled in the tea also act as a nice, slightly warming sweetener. If *pitta* is in excess, then choose maple syrup. For calming *vata*, use honey or raisins to sweeten tea. Adding ground nutmeg will also calm *vata*. Use a moderate amount, as it has a sedative quality.

TWICE⹀OVERS AND ONE⹀DISH

MEALS

LEFTOVERS

Leftovers (twice-overs) are not ideal. Reheating and overcooking destroys the remaining *prana* in the food. Refrigeration dries out the food and re-heating destroys any remaining *prana* rendering it nutritionally on par with cardboard. The safest timeframe for leftovers is around 4-6 hours, from lunch to dinner. If you are accustomed to making and eating leftovers, first work towards eating food within 24 hours of cooking it. Then work towards not eating leftovers beyond the next meal of that day. Eating food with more *prana*, life force, will have you feel better with a greater sense of well-being. Many people tell me that their level of energy increased notably when they stopped eating leftovers.

If you are not likely to cook twice in one day, try these combinations of **leftovers from the previous meal only**. The recipes can be referenced in their respective chapters.

Remember to eat slightly more augmenting foods than extractive. Sometimes you will need to cook an additional vegetable or grain to combine with the leftover in order to maintain the balance and quantity needed.

In the recipes below, combine your leftovers with the freshly cooked additions.

◌∽

TWICE~OVERS

Garbanzo veggie soup

preparation time: 10-15 minutes
Leftovers combined to make the soup:

- ⑥ Garbanzo beans with coconut (blended coconut meat in coconut water, sesame oil, asafoetida, powdered ginger, powdered coriander, powdered cinnamon, ground black pepper)
- ⑥ Chinese cabbage with zucchini (Chinese cabbage, zucchini, fresh grated ginger, fresh grated turmeric, mustard seeds, cumin seeds, black sesame oil)
- ⑥ Beets (ghee, fresh grated ginger, fresh cilantro, buttermilk)

Cooked additions to the soup:

- ⑥ Carrot, little kale, little collards, little celery, pearl barley, split mung
- ⑥ Ghee, pinch of mineral salt, asafoetida, fresh grated turmeric, fresh grated ginger, cumin powder

Pumpkin cabbage soup with chapati and hummus

preparation time: 15-20 minutes
Leftovers combined to make the soup:

- ⑥ Pumpkin squash (ghee, black pepper, fresh grated ginger, fresh grated turmeric, fresh parsley, mineral salt))

- ⑥ Kale with purple cabbage (fresh grated ginger, fresh grated turmeric, fenugreek, black pepper, fresh parsley, fresh basil, ghee)

Cooked additions to the soup:

- ⑥ Carrot, Chinese cabbage, cumin powder, fresh grated ginger, ghee, fresh ground black pepper, white basmati rice (cooked with mineral salt and few drops of ghee.)

On the side:

- ⑥ Chapati
- ⑥ Hummus

Vegetable dhal soup with coconut chapati and buttermilk

preparation time: 15 minutes
Leftovers combined to make the soup:

- ൬ Dhal with hijiki (ghee, hijiki, mineral salt, cumin seed, asafoetida)
- ൬ Broccoli, celery with Chinese cabbage (ghee, fresh grated ginger, fresh grated turmeric, mineral salt, coriander seeds, black pepper)
- ൬ Sweet potato in a crust

Cooked additions to the soup:

- ൬ 1 cup rooibos herbal tea, chopped fresh coconut or flakes, raw cashew, and cucumber (peeled, chopped, and seeded) cooked in ghee

On the side:

- ൬ Chapati using ⅓ coconut flour
- ൬ Buttermilk

Millet dhal soup with chapati

preparation time: 10-15 minutes
Leftovers combined to make the soup:

- ✆ *Millet with ginger (ghee, fresh grated ginger, mineral salt, cinnamon powder, black pepper); buckwheat may be substituted*
- ✆ Dhal (ghee, mineral salt, asafoetida, nori, cumin seed)
- ✆ Baked sweet potato

Cooked additions to the soup:

- ✆ Carrots, beet greens, fresh grated ginger, ¼ cup buttermilk, ground split mung, ghee

On the side:

- ✆ Chapati

Veggie barley soup with chapati

preparation time: 30 minutes
Leftovers combined to make the soup:

- ⑥ Barley (ghee, mineral salt)

- ⑥ Dhal soup with urud dhal (ghee, hijiki, mineral salt, cumin seeds, asafoetida, powdered turmeric, fresh grated ginger)

- ⑥ Pumpkin squash with nutmeg (ghee, nutmeg, cinnamon powder, 3 whole cloves or ¼ tsp powder, fresh cilantro)

Cooked additions to make the soup:

- ⑥ White basmati rice

- ⑥ Beets, beet greens, kale, ghee, fresh grated ginger, fresh grated turmeric, fennel seeds, fresh ground black pepper, fresh chopped basil, chopped cashews

On the side:

- ⑥ Chapati with ghee or honey
- ⑥ Clover or sunflower sprouts

Veggie adzuki soup

preparation time: 15 minutes
Leftovers combined to make the soup:

- ☙ Sweet adzukis (mineral salt, asafoetida, cinnamon, maple syrup, ghee, chai tea)
- ☙ Brown basmati rice (mineral salt, ghee)
- ☙ Mixed vegetables (zucchini, carrot)

Cooked additions to make the soup:

- ☙ Herbal chai tea
- ☙ Sweet potatoes simmered with cinnamon powder and ghee
- ☙ Collards and celery cooked in water with coconut oil, mustard seed, and mineral salt

Beet soup

preparation time: 5 minutes
Leftovers combined to make the soup:

- Ⓖ Beets and beet greens with spices
- Ⓖ Brown basmati rice

Additions to make the soup:

- Ⓖ Fresh cilantro
- Ⓖ Cottage cheese

Combine beets, greens, rice, and cottage cheese. Place ¼-½ of the mixture in a blender and blend to smooth consistency. Mix with the remaining beets and rice.

∾

ONE-DISH MEALS

One-dish meals are comforting and particularly balancing for *vata* dosha. Be sure the ingredients are 60% augmenting and 40% extractive. Limit the ingredients to one grain, one legume or nut, and two or three vegetables. Too many different items becomes challenging for the digestive fire. Prepare enough of each food at lunch and combine the ingredients for a dinner stew.

Vegetable buckwheat stew

serves 4 | preparation time: 45 minutes; with pressure cooker, 25 minutes | *Augmenting and Extractive*

- ✪ 1 ½ cups buckwheat
- ✪ 1 Tbsp olive oil
- ✪ 4 cups water
- ✪ 1 tsp mineral salt
- ✪ 1 ½ cups chopped broccoli
- ✪ 1 cup chopped green beans
- ✪ 1 cup chopped carrot
- ✪ ¼ cup fresh chopped parsley
- ✪ 1 tsp oregano
- ✪ ½ tsp fresh ground black pepper
- ✪ ¼ cup chopped pistachio or macadamia nuts

Combine buckwheat, olive oil, water, and mineral salt in a pot. Bring to a boil and reduce to simmer for 30 minutes. Add remaining ingredients and stir. Cover with a lid and simmer for 5-10 minutes. With a pressure cooker, bring buckwheat, olive oil, water, and mineral salt to pressure for 18 minutes. Stir in remaining ingredients when the pressure has released. Add a little extra water if desired. Close the pot and let it sit on a low temperature for 5-10 minutes.

Tip: Add 1 cup of fresh paneer (see "Light Meals, Sides, and Drinks) or ½-1 cup of cottage cheese to complete the meal.

Bulgur wheat, cucumber with baby tomato

serves 4 | preparation time: 20 minutes to 2 hours (depending on soak time) | *Augmenting*

- ⚕ 1 ½ cup bulgur wheat
- ⚕ ½-¾ tsp mineral salt
- ⚕ 3 cups water
- ⚕ 1 Tbsp ghee
- ⚕ 1 tsp cumin powder
- ⚕ ½ tsp fresh ground black pepper
- ⚕ 1 cucumber, peeled, seeded, and chopped
- ⚕ ⅓ cup fresh chopped mint
- ⚕ ¾ cup fresh chopped parsley
- ⚕ 1-2 cups fresh baby tomatoes (optional)
- ⚕ 15 drops fresh lime

Prepare the bulgur by soaking or cooking. Add the rest of the ingredients, stir and let sit 5 minutes. If you want it warm, cook the spices in ghee first, and then add the bulgur and water. Simmer covered for 15-20 minutes. After 10 minutes of cooking, add cucumber, mint, and parsley. Add garden-fresh baby tomatoes and lime at the end.

Tip: Bulgur does not require cooking. Soak 2-3 hours in water and it's ready. If you have weak agni, cooking is best.

BALANCED MEAL IDEAS

These meal suggestions are for lunch and dinner. Whenever possible, eat your main meal between 10 a.m. and 2 p.m. when *agni* is strongest. This is when the sun is highest in the sky to support digestion. There are recipes in this book for each of the components in the meals. Mix and match according to the vegetables available, personal needs, and season of the year. Remember, balance comes with meals of slightly more augmenting than extractive food. Warming foods during the cold time of year and more cooling foods in the hot season.

Wild rice with cashews | black eyed peas | corn off the cob | bok choy

Pumpkin or carrot soup | simple beet greens | chapati | avocado

Brown and wild rice | dhal with sea vegetable | pumpkin with pecans | chinese cabbage | avocado

White basmati rice | brown lentils with arame | spaghetti or acorn squash | sautéed greens

Brown rice and quinoa | sweet potatoes mashed with cinnamon | black eyed peas with black sesame oil | bok choy

White basmati rice with turmeric | beets with cauliflower | greens

Quinoa with pistachio | sweet potatoes mashed with nutmeg | green beans with cucumber

Bulgur wheat, cucumber with baby tomato

Brown basmati rice with saffron | squash with parsley | kale with black sesame oil

Sweet potatoes with fresh coconut meat | kale with ginger and turmeric | guacamole

Quinoa with turmeric | green beans with collards

Brown basmati rice | pumpkin squash | kale | purple cabbage * as Pumpkin cabbage soup

Brown basmati rice | kambalika | zucchini | beets with beet greens * as Beet soup

Quinoa with ghee | kambalika | sweet potatoes | broccoli with greens

Wild rice | kambalika | broccoli or collards with shredded carrot

White basmati rice with saffron | dhal (thicker) | beets with carrot | kale with fresh fennel

White basmati rice with turmeric | black eyed peas | parsnips | broccoli with Chinese cabbage

Brown basmati rice | dhal soup | dinosaur kale with carrot

Wild rice | sweet potatoes mashed with cinnamon | cabbage with collards

White basmati rice with turmeric | green beans with pecans | broccoli | cucumber with zucchini

Rice and dhal with turmeric *** | sweet potatoes with rose petals | broccoli with kale

Millet | adzuki beans | beets, beet greens with cottage cheese

Brown and wild rice | black lentils (urud dhal) | squash | cabbage with beet greens

Simple sushi: sushi rice | carrot with cucumber | green beans | tahini dressing | wasabi | avocado | chopped cilantro | chopped parsley | nori sheet *can substitute zucchini for vegetable or add broccoli*

White basmati rice with teff | dhal with nori | carrot ginger soup | collard greens

Brown basmati rice | garbanzo beans with coconut | beets | Chinese cabbage with zucchini *as Garbanzo veggie soup*

Brown and wild rice mix | sweet potatoes with herbal chai tea | broccoli with celery

Brown basmati rice | dhal with hijiki | sweet potato in a crust | broccoli, celery with Chinese cabbage *as Vegetable dhal soup with coconut chapati and buttermilk*

Sweet adzuki sushi: brown basmati rice | mixed vegetables | sweet adzukis | spicy tahini sauce | red clover sprouts | nori sheet | avocado | peeled and seeded cucumber sticks | ume plum paste | black sesame seeds

Bulgur wheat | garbanzos | pumpkin soup | purple cabbage with collard greens

Wild rice with dhal *** | beets, beet greens with fresh chopped cilantro and parsley | guacamole with dill

Millet with ginger | dhal | sweet potatoes | kale, collard greens with celery *as millet dhal soup with chapati*

Brown basmati rice | black eyed peas with black sesame oil | zucchini with purple cabbage

Barley | dhal soup with urud dhal | pumpkin squash with nutmeg | Chinese cabbage *as Veggie barley soup with chapati*

Rice with dhal *** | beets, beet greens with Japanese turnips (sweet)

Spicy rice | dhal | sweet potatoes with Chinese cabbage

White basmati rice | sweet potatoes mashed | green beans | cucumber with coconut

Quinoa with dhal *** | carrots with kale | avocado

Bulgur wheat with sesame oil | adzuki and garbanzo hummus | greens

Quinoa with turmeric | whole mung beans | beet soup

Brown and wild rice mix | black eyed peas | bok choy, carrots with zucchini

White basmati rice with turmeric | dhal with sea vegetable | kale, sweet turnips with red cabbage | serve with ½ cup of room temperature buttermilk

Brown rice | black lentils (urud dhal) | spiced carrots | simple beet greens

Quinoa with dhal | red cabbage with sweet turnip

White basmati rice | adzukis | carrots and fennel with kale

Barley with saffron | pumpkin squash | green beans with spinach

Brown basmati rice with saffron | dhal (thicker) | zucchini with broccoli

Red or brown rice | garbanzo beans with sesame oil | purple cabbage with celery | acorn squash

Spicy rice | hummus | okra with kale | chapati

See "Twice Overs and One Dish Meals" chapter for recipe.
**See "Twice Overs and One Dish Meals."*
***Find in "Legumes."*

Recipes for items such as wasabi, chapati, guacamole, and tahini dressings can be found in "Light Meals, Sides, and Drinks."

ABOUT THE AUTHOR

Myra Lewin is a wellness professional and educator in Ayurveda. A highly respected spiritual advisor and professional member of the National Ayurvedic Medical Association, she also trains Yoga teachers internationally with an emphasis on sustainable, conscious practice. She works extensively with clients in all phases of life and health. Myra lives on Kauai where she holds trainings, retreats, and grows her own delicious food on Durga Farms.

Myra Lewin has practiced, studied and taught Yoga, Ayurveda, nutrition, meditation, and energy management since the late 1980s. Her personal journey into the realm of healthy vegetarian eating and nature-based wellness began in the mid '70s.

Previously, Myra had a diverse career in the fields of medicine, executive management, and business consulting. Through Yoga and Ayurveda, Myra obtained complete healing from life-threatening diseases and has since guided many people from destructive habits to fulfilled and vital living.

Freedom in Your Relationship with Food: an Everyday Guide, Myra's first book, offers innovative practical guidance from the principles of Ayurveda and Yoga. Based on decades of working with others, it explains how to reawaken our innate connection with nature and our inner knowledge of what is best for our health.

Myra offers individual counseling, meditation retreats, teacher-trainings, workshops, and conference presentations around the globe. She is also an organic farmer, mediator, and minister in The Church of Aesclepion Healing. She works with people in any stage of life, including the elderly and those recovering from addiction. Her in-depth knowledge of human anatomy, physiology and psychology enables her to approach people at their level, encouraging the integration of healthy, balanced practices as a foundation for life.

With a focus on growth and service, Myra enjoys world travel, surfing, hiking and playing with her dogs.

She offers a wide variety of educational and experiential opportunities for students of all levels. Students' benefit from the example of her joy-filled life as much as from her teachings. Learn more at halepule.com.

Made in the USA
San Bernardino, CA
11 March 2017